CELINE

CELINE.COM

ISSEY MIYAKE

GRAIN DE CAFÉ
Cartier

SAINT-GERMAIN SOFA, PHOTOGRAPHED BY PAOLO ROVERSI

LE CLUB ARMCHAIR, PHOTOGRAPHED BY PAOLO ROVERSI

LUNCHEON

N.15 — SPRING SUMMER 2023   TABLE OF CONTENTS

CATCH OF THE DAY ⎰ Menu artwork created throughout the issue for *Luncheon* 15 by PZ Opassuksatit.

APERITIFS ⎰ PZRory Bargains…buying and selling bargains and lonely hearts with Gelitin, Claire Barrow, Sarah Andelman, Harry Freegard, Vaquera, Kiko Mizuhara and Joe Sweeney, pages 24–33.

SPECIALS ⎰ My Body is My Temple, photographed by Ekua King with make-up by Crystabel Riley, page 36 / Tablecloths by Jeremy Deller, Liam Sparkes and Sophie von Hellermann for Auction on behalf of Dora Brown, founded by Rebecca May Marston, page 48

MAIN DISHES ⎰ Polaroids by cinematographer Robby Müller selected by Andrea Müller-Schirmer, text by Evgeny Gusyatinskiy, page 58 / New York artist Jane Dickson in conversation with director, actor, writer and producer Sara Driver alongside a selection of paintings by Dickson, page 78 / Painter Alvin Armstrong in conversation with Reginald Moore, alongside a portfolio of his paintings and a portrait by Storm Harper, page 92 / Inspirations selected by the collective Ghetto Gastro with a conversation of explanations to the images between co-founder Jon Gray and friend and stylist Nell Kalonji, page 106

CLASSICS ⎰ Ulysses 100, poem and paintings by Art Hughes, page 130

DESSERTS ⎰ Lights Around, Sihana Shalaj photographed by Paolo Roversi in a Comme des Garçons special, styled by Robbie Spencer, page 136 / Couture, photographed by Nadine Ijewere, styled by Nell Kalonji and modelled by Divine Mugisha, page 148 / Scarecrows, photographed by Estelle Hanania, styled by Léopold Duchemin, initiated by Zoé Wirgin at the Lycée Paul Poiret, page 162 / By the Water's Edge, photographs by Jeano Edwards, styled by Hisato Tasaka, page 186 / New York New York A Bottle and a Cork, photographs by Cruz Valdez and styled by Marcus Cuffie, page 202 / The Holes in My Sweater, photographs by Bhumika Sharma and styled by Manglien Gangte, page 216

DIGESTIFS ⎰ A Short No Story by Hugh Corcoran, with a painting by Peter Doyle, page 238

THREE COVERS FOR LUNCHEON 15

Sihana Shalaj wears Comme des Garçons,
headpiece by Valeriane Venance
Photographed by Paolo Roversi, styled by Robbie Spencer, 2023

Kitchen. Kensington Motel, Santa Monica, Los Angeles
Polaroid by Robby Müller, 1985

Divine Mugisha wears Alaïa
Photographed by Nadine Ijewere, styled by Nell Kalonji, 2023

SONG OF THE ISSUE

TURTLES HAVE SHORT LEGS
by CAN

Turtles have short legs, not for the walking,
Turtles have short legs, not for the walking.

Want to have a cigarette, just king-sized,
Want to have a cigarette, just king-sized,
Well, we can find it out, well, we can find it out,
Well, we can find it out, well, we can find it out.

Turtles have short legs, not for the walking,
Turtles have short legs, not for the walking,
Well, we can find it out, well, we can find it out,
Well, we can find it out, well, we can find it out.
Want to have a cigarette, just king-sized,
Want to have a cigarette, just king-sized,
Well, we can find it out, well, we can find it out,
Well, we can find it out, well, we can find it out, ooh.

Turtles have short legs, not for the walking,
Turtles have short legs, not for the walking,
But we can find it out, but we can find it out,
But we can find it out, but we can find it out.
Want to have a cigarette, not for the choking,
Want to have a cigarette, just king-sized,
Well, we can find it out, well, we can find it out,
Well, we can find it out, well, we can find it out,
Well, we can find it out, well, we can find it out,
Well, we can find it out, well, we can find it out.

Well, we can find it out, well, we can find it out,
Well, we can find it out, well, we can find it out,
Well, we can find it out, well, we can find it out.

Produced by Can. Written by Damo Suzuki, Jaki Liebezeit, Holger Czukay,
Michael Karoli and Irmin Schmidt. Released 1971. From the album *Cannibalism 2* (1992).

CATCH OF THE DAY

MENU ARTWORK CREATED THROUGHOUT THE ISSUE FOR LUNCHEON 15 BY

PZ OPASSUKSATIT

PZtoday, *Fish Spoon and a Bad Manicure*, 2023
Photograph by Erick Faulkner, Le Dauphin restaurant, Paris

LIKE MUCH OF PZ'S WORK, YOUR MUNDANE ROUTINE TURNS ABSURD, EVERYDAY ITEM TURNS BIZARRE, IT'S BONKERS, IT'S IRONIC AND IT'S JUST SO PZTODAY!

THE ANIMALS
OBSERVATORY

APERITIFS

PZtoday, *A Room Service*, 2023
Photograph by Haotian Wang

PZ RORy BAR

Pound shop
Pawn
Bargains
WoW

****OPENING SOON!****

PZRORY BARGAINS

A New Pound Shop we need in Real life !

Business Brochure Special *by The Poundshop Owner :*
PZ Opassuksatit (PZtoday) and Rory Mullen
Shop Front photo by Peter Eason Daniels
Coming soon in 2023

PZRory BARGAINS

Overflowing buckets of sweeping brushes, garden mulch, various sizes of plastic tubs, dustbin full deflated footballs and sun bleached plastic flowers. Welcome to PZRORYBARGAINS - We will be stocking things like Claire Barrow's hot water bottles, Vaquera fly paper, Gelitins own brand dog poo poo bags, the list goes on and on. We display everything together which we think is fair! Everything is of equal value in PZRORYBARGAINS. High mixed with low. We like the idea of a little old woman coming in for some cat food and not realising its a unique artwork - she's feeds her cats and throws it in the recycling. PZRORYBARGAINS mixes the chaotic tradition of a pound shop with high end designer goods and cutting edge artists merchandise. **Ping** The customer has to decide which is which. You have to sift through a sea of bright colours and plastic packaging to discover what you hope is a gem.

What's PZRory Bargains?

Why you will love it?!

Our core values are -

Bargains are the best.

We use our brains to bargain for a job.

We use our energy to bargain for the cost of living.

We bargains our life, money and time for this project.

Why not come Bargains with us?

www.pzrorybargains.bigcartel.com

At PZRORYBARGAINS - We also have a pawn shop section - WOW - Artists and creatives or Joe Soaps can come to the counter and pawn their artworks in exchange for PZR's (our very own currency hehe) It's a win win situation - we get lots of interesting stock and the artists can make a crust. We have an expert in the back who decides how many PZRs the artwork is worth-and it's a brutal and market dependant! We pound we pawn ! We are creating a new way of displaying and distributing artwork and high fashion. An equal and fair way of giving the people what they want. Lots of love PZ+Rory x

WE BUY

ARTWORKS • GOODS • DESIGNERS
PZR Currency... How Does It Work?!

We accepted all Cashes, Cards, Cryptos, Artworks, Goods, Designers, Personal used items ...etc.

Trade!

WowoWwwww!

Convert to PZR Currency!

Buy! Buy! Buy!

Shopping!

WE SELL

GET PZR TOKEN TODAY @ WWW.PZRORYBARGAINS.BIGCARTEL.COM

BUY 2 PZR TODAY

GET 1 FREE

Wowwwooowwwww!

PZRory BARGAINS

CAVERNE D'ALI BABA

'I always love the feeling to be in a Caverne d'Ali Baba'
Sarah Andelman told us the secret location of where she goes to hunt for treasure! Follow us! In Rhinebeck, Upstate, The Stickle Family run "Al Stickle Five And Dime" since 1946 ! (read more...)

Meet PZRORY BARGAINS's Community : Claire Barrow (Photo by Daniel Swan), Sarah Andelman (Photo by Todd Selby), Harry Freegard (Photo by Peter Eason Daniels), Gelitin (Photo courtesy of Gelitin), Vaquera (Photo courtesy of The Fédération de la Haute Couture et de la Mode), Kiko Mizuhara (Photo courtesy of Kiko Mizuhara), Joe Sweeney (Photo by Rory Mullen), and Matty Bowan (Photo by Carlos Jiménez for NOW Gallery)

SARAH ANDELMAN
(Founder of Just An Idea / ex-Colette and A Covid Mask Trader)

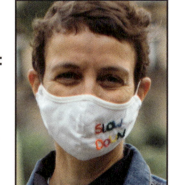

" I buy any kind of stuff: bandana, cleaning, toys…Covid Masks that I hope to never wear again? I have lots of boxes left ready to be trade at *PZRORY BARGAINS* !

HARRY FREEGARD
(Artist and A Pound Shop Connoisseur)

" Does CEX count as Pawn? I've too many memory of Poundshop!!!!! I'm a pound shop connoisseur, my favourites being the ropey independent ones, exquisite portals! However my most enduring poundshop memory has to be as a tween, deep into my Emo era being caught shoplifting fairy wings and eyeliner with my friends as we wanted to save our money to buy cinema tickets and needed something gorgeous to wear for the screening, five finger discount with our sticky fingerless gloved hands, alas, thwarted by a curt redhaired woman who's name I can only imagine was Sandra or Kelly, still dreaming of those wings.

GELITIN

A group of four artists from Vienna, Austria

> We tried poundshops to buy materials for setting up exhibitions, but everything we bought started to break. so we switched back to stealing materials from constructionsites and pick up free materials from friends and trash off the streets. Much better.

(From Left: Wolfgang Gantner, Florian Reither, Ali Janka and Tobias Urban.)

PZRory BARGAINS

Have you ever pawned anything?

We once pawned Ali. He spent the weekend in a basement in new jersey, USA. A rabbi we owed 74.- dollars chained him to some pipes and did beautifuls things to him all weekend long.

PATRIC DICAPRIO
(Founder of Vaquera, Dollar More Fanatic)

> We love "Dollar More" in China town, NY city. It's our little secret! From underwear, posters, food, little Statue of Liberty - Dollar More was a Fashion Awakening.

BRYN TAUBENSEE
(Founder of Vaquera, Trash connoisseur)

> Our dream is to pawn some Vaquera - having some of our finest pieces displayed in a pawn shop window. We want to be surprised. Disgusted and attracted.

Vaquera: Dear PZRORYBARGAINS customers - you should be excited about Vaquera's mystery trash bags that we're making - Will you get a custom piece?, some recycling? or dog poop? - You never know what you gonna get... It's all part of the fun!

CLAIRE BARROW
(CEO of Claire Barrow, Artist and a spooky toy trader)

> Poundshops are my favorite. It's a place I being allowed to pick a treat for myself.

SUPER WEEKEND DEAL AT PZRBARGAINS

CLAIRE BARROW'S
Spooky Doll
PZR
HS -9502 /PC.

100% Plant-Based
PZRORY's
Organic Compost
1 PZR
HS -3101 /PC.

PZRORY's
Lucky Cat
2 PZR
HS -9701 /PC.

VAQUERA'S
Collectible Trash
5 PZR
HS -3923 /PC.

PZRORY's Original items
PZRORY's
Mosquito Swatter
1 PZR
HS -8516 /PC.

PZRORY's
Lunch Box Set
2 PZR
HS -90922 /PC.

KIKO MIZUHARA
(Model, actress, artist and Poundshop Lover)

"For my first Valentine's Day, I got all the items at a 100 yen store, but I forgot to buy the stickers for the decorations, so I had to wrap them with duct tape that I had at home and couldn't make them very pretty. **Scooted or Booted?!** Definitely I'd pawn the scooter that I got during Covid! I only rode it once, that's enough.

PZRory BARGAINS
Buy ~~10~~ Get PZR **15**
~~10 PZR~~

www.pzrorybargains.bigcartel.com

HS -230910
1 PC.
~~from 2~~
PZR 1
SAVE 50%

pzrory's Cat Jittler

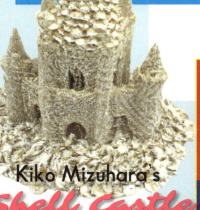
Kiko Mizuhara's Shell Castle
HS -03071190
1 PC.
~~from 6~~
PZR 4
SAVE 33%

pzrory's Kitchen Paper

HS -481820
1 PC.
~~from 2~~
PZR 1
SAVE 50%

PZRory BARGAINS

XXL

WWW.PZRORYBARGAINS.BIGCARTEL.COM

pzrory's Soccer Ball
HS -95066210
1 PC.
PZRORY's Original items
from ~~3~~
PZR **2**
SAVE 33%

Joe Sweeney's Salty Oyster Shell
HS -03071190
1 PC.
from ~~6~~
PZR **4**
SAVE 33%

pzrory's Vegan Chicken
HS -03071190
1 PC.
from ~~6~~
PZR **4**
BIO
SAVE 33%

JOE SWEENEY
(Artist and A Hardcore Pound)

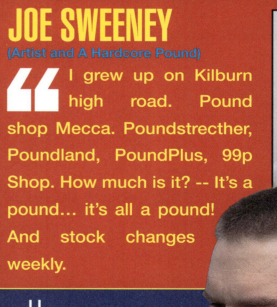

" I grew up on Kilburn high road. Pound shop Mecca. Poundstrecther, Poundland, PoundPlus, 99p Shop. How much is it? -- It's a pound… it's all a pound! And stock changes weekly.

Joe Sweeney's Tea Pot
HS -6909
1 PC.
Joe's Original items
from ~~30~~
PZR **15**
SAVE 33%

CARD PAYMENT ONLY

Have you ever pawned anything ?

I am into hardcore Pawn. Cash converters to be precise. Today, I'm bringing a ceramic oyster shell, an ashtray, a salt dish, a lifestyle!

BUY PZR CURRENCY TODAY 2 GET 1 FREE @ WWW.PZRORYBARGAINS.BIGCARTEL.COM

PZRory BARGAINS

MATTY BOWAN
(Designer, Artist and a Natural Born Poundshopper)

"I don't remember a time without poundshops - some of my early work was made with all stuff from the poundshop, I like items on mass, and I like glittery hair accessories and cheap nail polish that stinks your house out, and bootleg dvds from the poundshop, press on nails and plastic tablecloths. -- I want to find the unexpected. In the world of homogeny, I want to be shocked and turned on by shopping, I do get obsessed by certain colours and will buy several things if I like the colour in that moment.

AND THAT'S MATTY BOWAN GUYS !

We are still looking for sponsorship and collaborators - Get in Touch -
PZRORYBARGAINS@GMAIL.COM

SEE YOU SOON... X PZRORY BARGAINS

LUNCHEON lonely heart

Abbreviations
- **JLFTR** - Just looking for the ride.
- **SGS** - Still gums speed.
- **HLAAR** - Hairline leaving at an alarming rate.
- **HS** - Heavy smoker.
- **HD** - Heavy drinker.
- **PWOS** - Possible waft of shite.
- **WLTM** - Would like to meet.

0122 AGING PUNK
Recently widowed aging punk. Seeks friendship of more. HS HD SGS. Who will rock my Casbah!?

0222 WEALTHY KERRY MAN IN LONDON
Hard working retired builder JLFTR

0322 FRIENDLY FARMER
Pig farmer PWOS. Friends call me Mick the dick. WLTM Pretty lady with Christian values. Looking for friendship and sauciness. Give me a bell!

0422 SWEDISH GENTLEMAN
Fat-ish jolly man HLAAR. WLTM man for friendship, over 70s, gets lonely sometimes, meals out, Bruce Springsteen music, short walks(bad leg), must have car, address and no phone please.

0522 SEANY CALLING
Offaly nice man, easy going, caring gent, kind natured, love all kind of music within reason, NS, likes simple things in life, So come on ladies! Seany is your man.

1090 TRULY MADLY DEEPLY
URGENT Searching a soul mate. Tik-tok Tik-tok - Time running out, JLFTR, HD, Hard core pounding. Psychic alarming - Last chance

1112 SHOP INVESTOR
Don't miss a chance to become a billionaire. A MILF and a DILF looking for a life-time investor coolest shop of your corner. No commitment.

LAST BUT NOT LEASE...
I'VE GOT SO MUCH TO TELL YOU...
LADY HARRY !

As our readers know - our resident agony aunt is here to answer any difficult questions. Be that getting in touch with a departed loved one or help sifting through the chaff of life - Harreth is here to help. Using tea cups, magic balls and star charts - your questions will be answered.

Sarah from Chorley: My husband Ian died last year and ever since we think he's be attempting to 'haunt' the house - can you ask him to stop? **- He says Don't flatter yourself**

Mark from Truro: We bought an ouija board on Ebay but when it arrived it was an ouija pattern printed on some men's swimming trunks - can these still be used to contact the dead? **- Only when the wearer is erect**

Brian from Clacton-on-sea: My wife has recently started wearing a trilby at a jaunty angle when we go out on the weekends. can you offer some advice please. **- Manifest Strong winds.**

Charles from Birmingham: My mother had a drinking problem and her last question to the doctor was 'is there an off licence in the afterlife' - I hope you can help **- Rest assured there's one on every corner and they still do 50p charge on card payments under £5.**

Chico from Inverness: Harry - my uncle was lost at sea. Can you help our family get closure. **- He likes it out there, let people enjoy things.**

To have your question answered by Harry please text 07864905572 - **Help me harry! 1PZR / per convo.**

Business Brochure Special by PZ Opassuksatit (PZtoday) and Rory Mullen - 2023 ©

PZtoday, *Delivery in Shanghai*, 2023

SPECIALS

MY BODY IS MY TEMPLE

**PHOTOGRAPHS BY
EKUA KING**

**MAKE-UP BY
CRYSTABEL RILEY**

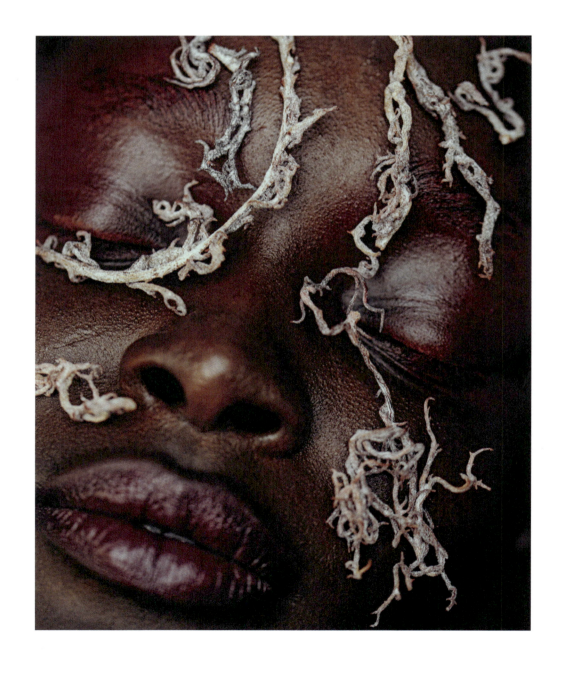

Models JAMES CORBIN at SUPA, SIMI BUCCIARATI at BLUE AGENCY, BABA GUEYE at PRM,
AYUOL MANYOK at MILK, TASHA MALEK at FIRST • *Set Designer* SAMUEL PIDGEN • *Casting Director* THEO SPENCER
Photography Assistant ARTHUR COMELY • *Make-Up Assistants* TEMI ADELEKAN and TINA KHARTI

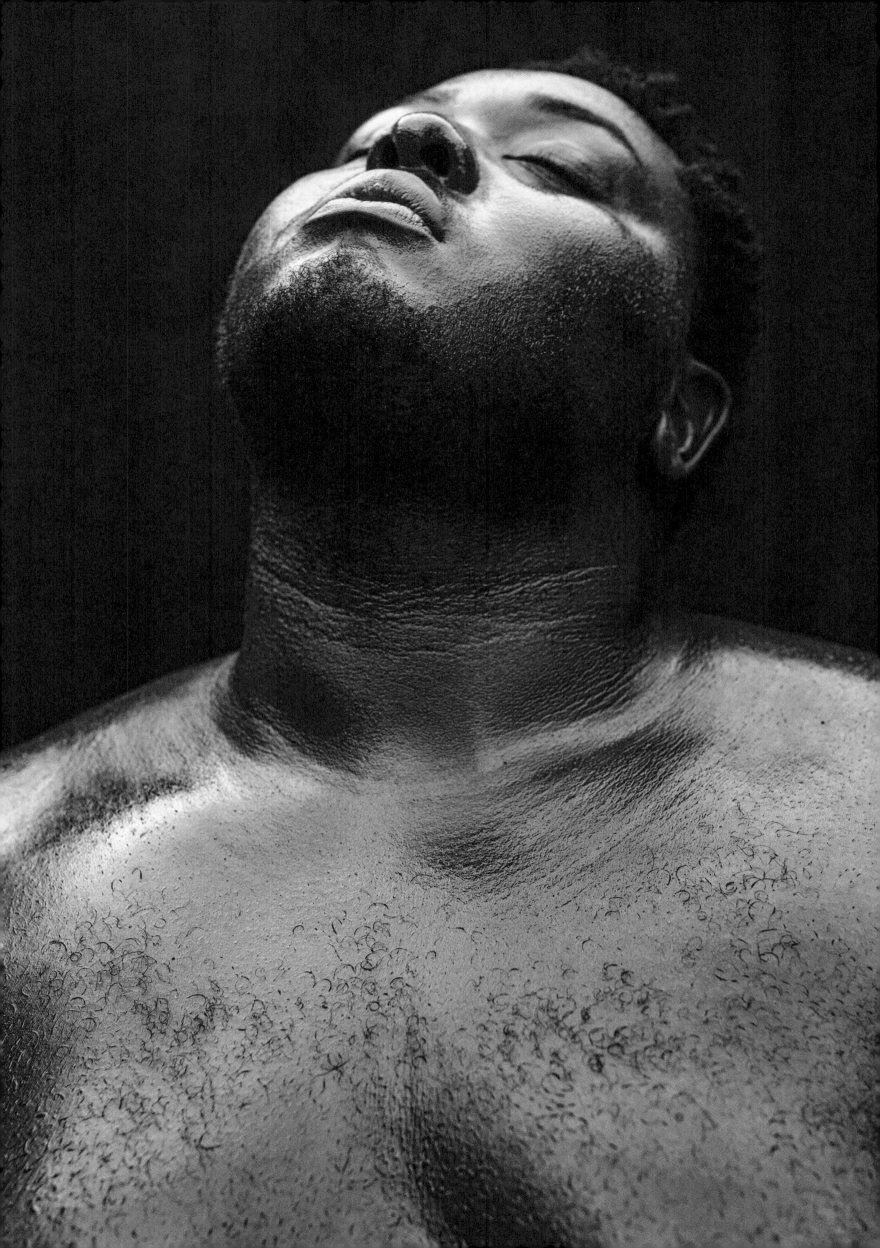

I was brought up in a Jamaican vegetarian/vegan family, whose mantra was 'Your Body is Your Temple'. Some of us are veggie, some are vegan. My family have been vegan since the 70s, way before being vegan became popular. I was raised vegetarian by my mother, who is all about natural and clean eating. It made me stick out a lot at school for my incredible packed lunches – a flask of stew peas, dumpling, steamed veg, green banana and plantain (at the time, you just want to be like everyone else with a jam sandwich…). My grandma would give all of my cousins and me a shot of aloe vera during the half term and holidays. Or if we weren't going anywhere the next day, we'd drink Irish moss, sometimes rub charcoal on our teeth before or after toothpaste. I've always had really bad hay fever so my mum always got me locally sourced honey (nothing to do with being Jamaican) for my hay fever which SAVES MY LIFE. – Ekua King

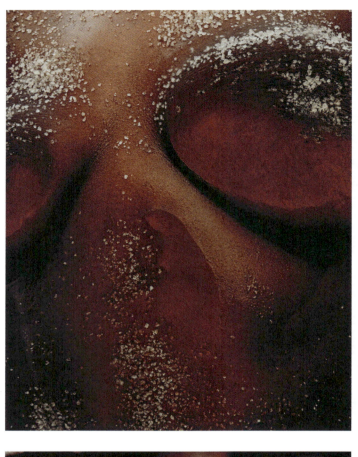

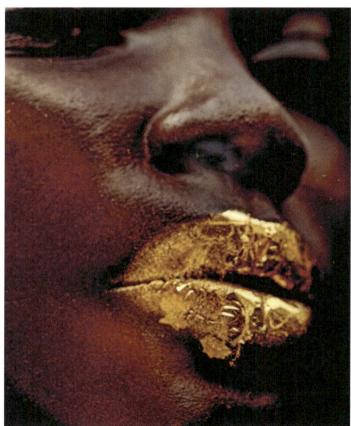

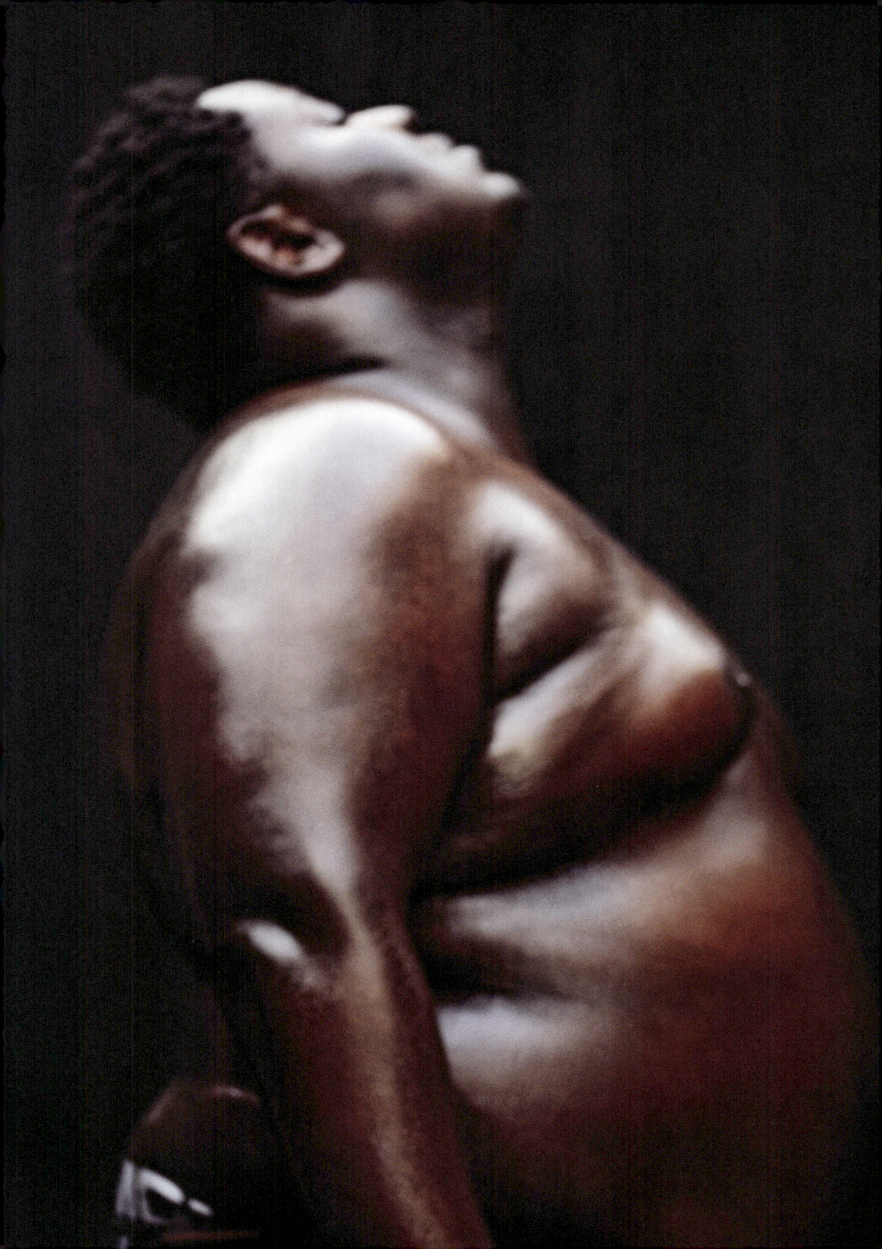

ART FOR DORA: TABLECLOTH AUCTION

WORDS BY REBECCA MAY MARSTON

Photographs taken from @dorabrownhomemaking Instagram

DORA BROWN IS A SOCIAL ENTERPRISE TRANSFORMING HOMES FOR WOMEN AND FAMILIES IN NEED, BASED IN SUFFOLK. A LARGE TEAM OF VOLUNTEERS TRANSFORM HOMES, FREE-OF-CHARGE, FOR FAMILIES LIVING IN CRISIS; HOMES WHICH HAVE BROKEN DOWN BECAUSE OF CONDITIONS, HYGIENE POVERTY AND DOMESTIC NEGLECT. WWW.DORABROWN.COM

Can we start at the end? With a thank you to the artists here. Artists are generous people, putting their ideas-made-real into the world and saying unquestioning yeses to favours. This favour means a lot to a lot of people; it literally, immediately changes the lives of families living in crisis in the UK. So, thank you Jeremy, Liam and Sophie.

Back to the start…Dora Brown is a beast, a fledgling charity helping families who are living in some of the worst home conditions in Britain. Every home is the next shittest thing and saddest situation; every home smells fetid, has pest issues, has kids or their parents sleeping on sofas, has no bedding, has schools reporting hygiene concerns about the kids' clothes and bodies not being washed, has no working oven nor washing machine, no dining table, no books, no toys. Dora's volunteer army (now numbering 80+ in our second year) turns it around for these families week after week, home after home.

We clear hoarding and rubbish piled floor to ceiling, deep-clean aged grot and mould, and organise other people's pants, ablution solutions and other stuff. Whatever the catalysts and contributors for decline, the weight of the chaos is paralysing for the families, and so it spirals until we spend hefty hours sorting, scrubbing and giving a shit about, and for, these families who are referred to us by social workers.

After clearance and cleaning comes provision: beds, mattresses, dining tables, chairs, bedding, lamps, cushions; things that every home and every person in that home should have. Dora flexes her DIY, installing curtains and blinds, mirrors and hooks. She carpets, replacing bare chipboard and concrete floors. She makes homes function: unblocking toilets and installing washing machines; she resets the laundry mountains to zero; she donates cleaning equipment and hoovers, laundry and bathroom products. Dora gifts fruit bowls and artworks and books and toys and vases. She makes homes to be proud of and thrive in. It works. Her families start letting friends cross the threshold. Teachers report proud, happier, cleaner, well-slept kids. Social workers remove children from Child Protection Plans.

Dora's a big team of volunteers, recruited largely from the most powerful demographic in (un)employment: school parents. It's sad, intense and grim-as-sin work, but Dora in action is joy. The m.o. is non judgmental, caring not for what is uncovered, and kindness towards our families. Somehow, it's fun. (I once wet myself: it was a really bad home, one of the first, when my founding partner and best mate, Sacha, and I, took the worst jobs for ourselves. It was a third floor toilet that had had a can of paint thrown down it by two of the ten kids. They had carried on using it and it was nigh-on full of brown, with flies circling. We found a rusty thermos and started scooping it out, retching…until I wet myself. A bit. I went to find some loo paper in the only working toilet, meanwhile Sacha filled the other with bleach then flushed it; it refilled with fizzy brown and she called a plumber. He cleared it in four minutes. Never again. Never. Again.) (I checked in on a new volunteer recently who was excited to get to her veterinary job the next day, hoping for some rotten anal glands to get the smell of the family homes out of her senses.)

Aside from Dora in all her altruistic, gruesome, delicious brilliance, there's resourcing her work. A lot is donated in time, money and stuff from our corporate partnerships and supporters, but we also need cash. Back to beautiful artists being wonderful people and us asking a few to make tablecloths to auction. One, because art is actually my home not social care; and two, because context is everything and artworks as tablecloths or tablecloths that are art, for a homemaking charity having to provide families with a table and chairs to eat at, is mischievous tomfuckery. Three artists + art + auction + charity = an alchemy of greatness.

Here's the first round of Art for Dora's fundraising: Jeremy Deller, Liam Sparkes and Sophie von Hellermann. Follow our socials and silently bid to win one this June. Thanks at the end then, too.

Rebecca May Marston, founder director of Dora Brown, Suffolk. Previously Limoncello Gallery, London.

Bidding via DM to @ArtForDora or email to dora@dorabrown.com
from Wed 15th June 9am closing Thu 16th June 9pm.

LIAM SPARKES

Liam Sparkes, *Ship Tablecloth*, 2023, embroidered linen, 250 x 150 cm
Courtesy of the artist. Photograph by Danny North

JEREMY DELLER

Jeremy Deller, *Marmite on Toast*, 2023, acrylic on linen, 250 x 150 cm
Courtesy of the artist. Photograph by Julia Bostock

SOPHIE VON HELLERMANN

Sophie von Hellermann, *Angels at My Table*, 2023
Acrylic on linen, 250 x 150 cm
Courtesy of the artist and Pilar Corrias Gallery
Photographs by Ollie Harrop

MAIN DISHES

PZtoday, *La Tour Eiffel Leftover*, 2023
Photograph by Erick Faulkner, Le Dauphin restaurant, Paris

POLAROIDS BY ROBBY MÜLLER

Selected by

ANDREA MÜLLER-SCHIRMER

Every time I look at Robby's Polaroids I see them in a new light. The photographs show his incredibly brilliant eye for everyday details and how light brings things to life. For this series of his Polaroids, I wanted to create the atmosphere of an intimate, modest and serene world, a mood that suits Robby. – Andrea Müller-Schirmer

ALL IMAGES © Robby Müller Archive/Annet Gelink Gallery, Amsterdam

KITCHEN

Kensington Motel, Santa Monica, Los Angeles, June–July 1985

COFFEE MAKER

Kensington Motel, Santa Monica, Los Angeles, June–July 1985

A PERMANENT LIGHT

THE POLAROIDS OF ROBBY MÜLLER

by

EVGENY GUSYATINSKIY

When you first see the Polaroids of Robby Müller, you might not guess that they were made by one of the greatest cinematographers of all time. A close collaborator of Jim Jarmusch, Wim Wenders and Lars von Trier (to mention just a few), Müller made an invaluable contribution to their works, most of which are considered masterpieces.

The difference in scale is what may strike us at first glance: a tiny Polaroid with fixed dimensions stands even further apart from the theatrical big screen than a classic analogue photograph, which can come in different formats.

As a cinematographer, Müller created images so rich and emblematic that it has never been enough just to look at them. You want to be a part of them, to be there among those people, landscapes and narratives; they are so similar to reality, yet so different. And they welcome you in.

Müller's Polaroids engage us in a different way, as they bring the actual world, so familiar and yet unnoticed, closer to our eyes. While Müller's films transport us to another world inside the screen, his Polaroids are like postcards sent to us to (re)connect us with the universe we live in, the one that already belongs to us. Perhaps here lies one of the general differences between photography and film.

The older Müller's oeuvre gets, the more iconic and contemporary it becomes. This is probably the classic paradox of a genius: establishing or rather revealing and shaping an artistic canon without any intention to do so, creating timeless presence out of transience, even out of absence. Isn't that also the basic, original intent of every (still and moving) image?

A hollow Christmas bauble lying on the floor. Half a peeled orange. A coffee maker on the stove. A variety of glass bottles, empty, half-empty or turned into vases with flowers in them. The poetry of ordinary things and common places. In fact, this resonates with the medium itself, as Polaroids originated and became popular as everyday objects, mostly circulating outside the world of museums and galleries.

Like everyone else back then, Robby Müller was probably lured by the joyful magic of the Polaroid camera. It accompanied him on his travels and on shoots, at home and at work. However, he never used it to film the shooting process or behind-the-scenes moments; he used it for his own pleasure, not intending to make the images public. The accessibility and easiness of the Polaroid, which made it a mass-market commodity, are present in Müller's pictures too, lending them a dimension of humanness and openness, especially when compared to the 'high-brow' nature of his films.

You can almost feel that he made these images alone at home, or in a hotel room, contemplating his close surroundings, distracting himself from the outside world, away from the buzz and crowds of the film set. A daily ritual of solace, encouraging a moment of solitude that is so understandable and relatable.

These images bear no presence of human beings, except Robby Müller himself, invisible, hidden behind the camera, his fingerprints most likely covering the surface of his Polaroids. On a couple of occasions he enters the frame by filming his hand holding half an orange or by taking a snapshot of his own shadow. Yet the intimacy and tranquillity of these works bears no relation to the intrinsic amateur aesthetics of Polaroid that preceded the era of home video.

One could argue that the invention of Polaroid was the first step towards the culture of Instagram, a culture in which the ceaseless production of instant images has become part of everybody's routine and has triggered a certain inflation of the medium. Most of the myriad of online images within this culture seem the same and interchangeable. Being very much aware of the specifics and effects of Polaroid technology, Müller subverted or advanced it by resorting to its very own means. After all, his snapshots are much closer to paintings, particularly to *nature mortes*, as they reveal the imminent stillness of the world that precedes movement.

As a visionary artist, Müller turns on its head the classic idea (and ideal) of photography, especially that relevant to Polaroid. He is not setting in stone a certain moment in time, cutting it out from the flow of an unstoppable movement, or saving it from oblivion. Instead, his Polaroids show that not everything exists in movement and not everything is dependent on time. There are things that prevail by being indifferent to the harrowing machinery of time and movement, but sometimes they don't look like that at all. Like the view from a window in New York. Like the choreographic interplay of light and shadow that repeats itself daily in a room.

Much has been said about Müller as a grandmaster of light, who captured the very essence of its elusive, abstract nature. Indeed, his Polaroids are struck by a ray of light emanating from inside the image to its surface, to the viewer, leaving the frame and lighting an actual physical space beyond it. Besides, many of the objects in his photographs are completely transparent. Basically, they are rendered as containers of light that make it even more visible. Light is transient (it appears and disappears), while transparency is permanent (it stays and persists). Along with stillness, transparency creates a sense of wholeness, uniting things of different shapes, materials and purposes.

Robby Müller's Polaroids may look like they are made spontaneously, without a second thought, perhaps taking only one frame at a time. But what they represent is far from spontaneity: a world of tranquillity, silence and resilience, a world that existed long before the arrival of the photographer, even before the invention of the medium. And it will stay like that even after the artist leaves. Unchanged and undisturbed.

Eternity, a grand concept that seems far removed from the lightness and sensuality of Robby Müller's style, and even further from the nature of Polaroid, is already here: it's in our rooms, on our tables, next to our windows. And there is no need, for an artist or for us as viewers, to create another one.

LA PALMA

September, 1984

STILL LIFE

La Palma, March–April 1985

SHADOW OF SELF-PORTRAIT

La Palma, 1987

GRAMERCY PARK HOTEL

New York City, April 1981

PASTIS BOTTLE

La Palma, September–October 1987

APPLE

Taormina, 1987–88, while filming *Il Piccolo Diavolo*

RED GERANIUM IN BOTTLE WITH SHADOW

La Palma, September–October 1987

BOTTLE WITH LOVE-IN-A-MIST

Lindos, Rhodes, August 1980

STILL LIFE WITH LEAF AND GREEN GLASS BALL

Munich, c. 1985

ORANGE

Munich, 1981

ASHTRAY AND LAMP

Kensington Motel, Santa Monica, Los Angeles, 1984 or 1985,
while filming *To Live and Die in L.A.*

GRAMERCY PARK HOTEL

New York City, Room 605, November 1988

HONEY BEAR

Mayflower Hotel, New York City, 1988

MIRRORED HONEY BEAR

Mayflower Hotel, New York City, 1988

INDIAN CRESS AND OTHER FLOWERS IN A VASE

La Palma, 1988

DESK AT HOME

Munich, May 1984

JANE DICKSON AND SARA DRIVER IN CONVERSATION

Ahead of her exhibition in London, New York painter Jane Dickson talks with her friend Sara Driver the director of the films Boom for Real: The Late Teenage Years of Jean-Michel Basquiat, You are Not I, Sleepwalk *and* When Pigs Fly, *and producer of* Stranger than Paradise *and* Permanent Vacation *(directed by Jim Jarmusch), she recently won the Special Jury Prize for Screenwriting Sundance 2022 for the animation* Stranger than Rotterdam *by the Kloster Brothers. Over lunch in Dickson's studio in Brooklyn, the two long time friends discuss Times Square of the 1970s and 80s, the artists who passed through and the influences it had on their work and life up till today.*

OPPOSITE — Jane Dickson and Sara Driver photographed by Edwin Almanzar
FOLLOWING PAGE — Jane Dickson photographed by Sara Driver

SARA DRIVER: Do you get to see many shows?

JANE DICKSON: I don't see as many shows as I want, but I try to, it's important. Same way you go see movies, right?

SARA: Yeah, absolutely. That's how we learn, from other people. And did you see the Hopper show [*Edward Hopper's New York*, Whitney Museum of American Art, 2022-23]?

JANE: I did see the Hopper show. I did some of the commentary for the Hopper show. And I'm going to be on a panel in two weeks to talk about the Hopper show at the Whitney.

SARA: It's natural that you would be, with your work and the way you use light and shadow. When I was reading about you, one of the artists your work led me to was [American printmaker] Martin Lewis, who did etchings in the 30s and 40s. Your work seems closer aligned with his than almost anybody's I've seen. You also talk a little bit about being influenced by the Japanese artist Hokusai.

JANE: I remember a curator coming to my studio once, and saying, 'Oh, your work makes me think of Martin Lewis'. And at the time, I didn't know who that was. But then I looked it up and went, yeah, that totally makes sense.

SARA: I love those figurative drawings from the 30s and 40s…they have a kind of fluidity, like a movement to them.

JANE: Back to your question of do I go see shows…I feel like my job as an artist is to be a part of the dialogue of my times, or that is the artist's role I have chosen. I'm not interested in going to the top of the mountain and communing with God and then coming back to show the world the Ten Commandments. It's fantasy; I feel like a lot of artists are like, I'm just gonna go to my studio and paint for the next 30 years and then the world will go, Oh my God, you're just what we were waiting for. I feel like I'm interested in art being the basis of a conversation, a dialogue about whatever is really important about our time and place.

SARA: I love your paintings of garages!

JANE: Thank you. The garages, the highways and *Lucky Food* shopping plazas all relate to my suburban youth. I was born and raised in the suburbs of Chicago till I was 14. But my heart was really in the city, and I couldn't wait to get here when I was young. My parents got divorced when I was 15 and I got sent to boarding school in Vermont, hippie school. That was the late 60s, early 70s.

SARA: Very few families were divorced at that time. It was unusual, actually.

JANE: True. Before her divorce, I remember my mother warning me never to marry someone from a divorced family. That it would cause lots of problems. Well, hers solved some problems but caused many more. My parents had spent their adolescence and early adulthood during World War Two. So when the 1960s happened, and they had four kids, a dog and a bunch of parakeets, they looked at each other and looked around and went, Hey, this swinging 60s thing looks like fun. So they split up; my mother moved to Paris and my father moved to Miami with his secretary. We kids were mostly on our own. We bounced back and forth between them and all over with friends. My parents had no idea where we were or what we were doing. My mother didn't ask what I was going to do until my high school graduation. When I said I didn't know she invited me to stay with her in Paris and go to the Ecole des Beaux-Arts for a year. One of the rare times she stepped up.

SARA: How old were you?

JANE: 18. And while I was there, I applied to Harvard because my older brother was there. I thought, if he can do it, I can do it. That was the only place I applied. And they accepted me. I have no idea what my life would have been if it hadn't worked out that way. After I finished college in Boston, I got hired to teach there the year I graduated. I was hired as a teaching assistant but there was no teacher so I was teaching lithography the year I graduated, which was insane. But I couldn't wait to get out of Boston so when that year ended, I drove to New York. I had studied animation and my animation teacher was Susan Pitt. She hired me the day I got here.

SARA: She did wonderful animations. I met her once at the MoMA.

JANE: I painted many of those cells. My first job in New York was painting cells for Susan on Broadway. Susan was, like, ten years older than me and she was friends with [American multimedia artist] Red Grooms and [Swiss-American filmmaker/photographer] Rudy Burckhardt so she introduced me to this network of artists. I remember meeting Red Grooms and he was like, 'Welcome, if you are crazy enough to want to come be part of the scene, join us.' The art world was so small then. You were probably in New York by then, right? This was 77 I think.

SARA: That's when I landed in New York after college. And what was wonderful too is how we had no ageism, we were hanging out with these older artists who were our parents' age, like [Swiss photographer/documentary filmmaker] Robert Frank, [American poet] Allen Ginsberg or Red Grooms, or [American painter/sculptor] June Leaf (see *Luncheon* No.11). And we were all going to the same parties and it was wonderful – there was no kind of feeling of anybody's age at all. It was more about art, and ideas.

JANE: And when I came to New York in my mid-20s, the basis of my work was already there. I have some early images, even from high school, that are so much like what I have continued to do. But I hadn't really clarified it consciously yet to myself, and I wanted to be hip. And I kept thinking, maybe I'll learn to be abstract.

SARA: I was going to ask you about that, because that's what was happening in the art world in the 70s. Figurative hadn't quite come back.

JANE: People were hardly painting at all in Paris, but if they were it had to be abstract and I remember even in high school thinking, Must I? The reason I left Harvard and went to the Boston Museum school is because it was like fourth-generation Bauhaus. They really didn't want you to look at anything or draw from a model, they wanted you to talk about your theory – it was all about process. So I went to the museum school where they taught life drawing, which I really wanted to be able to do because I felt like on some level, my paintings were smoke signals of what's real. Particularly because both my parents were extreme fantasists who I felt were trying to convince me that bullshit was real and reality was bullshit. And I would be like, 'No, really, the sun rises in the morning, and the moon is out at night. And you can tell me as many times as you want that the opposite is true, but I can see it.'

SARA: When did you introduce photography, because you paint from photographs?

JANE: I did take a couple of photography classes in high school. I loved the magic of the dark room, where you see the image emerge in the bath – black and white photography, I was totally transfixed by it. And I think the way that I paint is referencing that always, where I start on a middle tone or a dark ground and then gradually start with light layers of colour that are very close to the background. Then I'll put another layer on another layer till

Jane Dickson, *Empire Sign Changing 3*, 2020, acrylic on linen, 91.4 x 55.9 x 3.2 cm
Courtesy of Alison Jacques, London © Jane Dickson; photograph by Paul Hodara

it emerges. But I didn't want to be a photographer – that seemed too mechanical. I like to get my hands messy. After I finished working for Susan, and her film *Asparagus* was finished and being premiered at the Whitney, I started looking for animation jobs. I had all these ridiculous job interviews where the guy would be like, 'I can't give you a job but do you want to have dinner?'

SARA: That's what it was like in the 70s.

JANE: Yeah, I don't want to hire you, but I want to sleep with you. So I saw an ad in the *New York Times* for animators willing to learn computers. This is 78. And it was for the first digital lightboard. In Times Square, it was the first digital lightboard in New York, maybe in the country. So I went and they hired me and at the end of the interview they're like, 'Of course you can type, right?' And I said, 'Of course!' I had gotten all the way through college refusing to type because my stepmother wanted me to go to typing school and be a friggin secretary like she was. I bought a teach-yourself-to-type-book and spent the weekend practising until my fingers were numb.

SARA: Were there a few animators or just you?

JANE: I think there were four or five of us, because they always needed someone to be manning the lightboard sign when it was running. So I worked the night shift on weekends, because I didn't want to interrupt my studio time in the day. I had done nightshift jobs in college too, for some reason I thought I was a night owl. And you know, why did I think this was a good idea of a job? It was like I was a moth to the flame. I felt like it was really interesting. I had had such a dysfunctional childhood and I think I wanted to not be at all domestic, because I think my mother really focused on it and was very unhappy. So I thought living in a former abortion clinic on 43rd Street with Charlie was so not domestic, it was perfect. We had a hot plate and a little mini fridge so we really couldn't think about cooking. That seemed great to me.

SARA: You must have seen amazing things at night. Going to work, coming home from work.

JANE: I carried this little Minox to just shoot from my hip wherever I went. I took photos on the street, out the window where I lived on 43rd Street and from the windows at work behind the lightboard sign. I used autofocus because my eyesight isn't so great and because I was often shooting in tense situations where I didn't want people to see that I was shooting. I did quick sketches from the window but they were very loose and generalised. Sometimes I got friends to recreate a pose for me to photograph later to give me more detail to work with. I got little drugstore prints, because I wanted to be clear to myself that I wasn't trying to make artful photos, these were always notes towards paintings.

In those days there were lots of trans-gender people (then called transvestites) on 43rd Street. We lived above Sally's Hideaway, one of the first voguing clubs, where they shot *Paris Is Burning*. They would spill out of the club at 3 or 4am and get into fights under our window and the cops would come break it up almost every night. When I was on the street there was a lot to navigate, between the dudes at my studio door hawking 'coke, speed, valium' or the old drunks shouting 'pull your pants down bitch'. And we got our windows shot in.

SARA: You got your windows shot in?

JANE: Twice! From two different sides. There were two times when I was in my little living room on the corner and a bullet came through the window. I don't know if anyone was actually aiming at us, or whether they were just shooting off a gun, but it was a terrifying place to live, honestly.

SARA: But you had both of your children there.

JANE: Yes, God help them. I didn't plan to have children in Times Square. But it was a moment when things were getting more and more expensive, and we couldn't afford to move. And life happens you know. Our building was finally condemned for the Times Square Redevelopment in 1992 so we had to move downtown then.

SARA: Let us go back to the Times Square lightboard sign – that really informed your work in many ways. Maybe you could talk a little bit about why – because of your use of textures, your use of light and shadow, it seems like that lightboard sign was the beginning of it.

JANE: Yes, because I was looking at digital signs for my job. And I had done a little graphic design and was interested in typefaces. And when I started working at the sign, the only typeface that was available was Unicode. They hadn't designed any others. So anytime we would get an ad like Coca Cola and needed to do it in the Coke serif font, I would have to make it. I would have to do the word 'Coke' but then while I was at it, I'd do the rest of the alphabet and save it so that the next time anybody wanted to use that type, we already had it.

SARA: How long did you do that job for?

JANE: I think four years. By 1982 my colleagues on the sign were moving out to LA to start a special effects company and they invited me to come with them. And I thought, Hmmm, 21st century doing special effects in Hollywood, or 19th century doing oil paintings in New York? I'm going with my heart to the 19th century materials. I loved the smell and feel of paint. The computer was too cold. I kept wanting to put my hand into the screen to move things around, to blend them. Especially in that era, you really had to plan everything out and do frame one, frame two, frame three. It just lacked the sensual, textural thing that makes me extremely happy making art. I was showing at Fun Gallery (the only woman to ever have a show there), I was getting some attention, I was getting support, and I was selling work. And I thought maybe I can really do this.

SARA: But it's interesting, too, that you lived in the Times Square area all through the 80s.

JANE: Till the end of 92. I kept a studio there until 2008. I had a studio on 39th and 9th, which is methadone central. All I can guess is that having been on my own since I was 14, and having had a lot of family members with substance issues, I was just totally in denial. I loved going to the Mudd Club but I never stayed for the after-after parties because I couldn't stand drugs. I thought it was a character failure on my part that I couldn't really get into smoking cigarettes, drinking that much or doing drugs, but it made me want to throw up and run away screaming.

SARA: We were talking about age, that there was no real evidence of people's ages. Was it the same with being male or being female? Being in the hip-hop world and being an artist, and being female. Did you feel like there was no boundary?

JANE: Well, the whole world was blindly sexist, racist and homophobic then. I joined Colab [Collaborative Projects] in 1978. It was better than most of the art world in that it included lots of powerful women artists but still women did most of the grunt work and men took most of the credit. I made friends with Kiki Smith and [American neo-conceptual artist] Jenny Holzer. It was sort of my grad school. People would propose projects, anyone could participate so it felt like trying on your friends' clothes. Like what work could I make for Jenny's *Manifesto Show*? Or Robin Winters' *Doctors and Dentists Show*? I'd put something up and see how people reacted. There was a little bit of money from the city that mostly the women had applied for so there was just enough to make it worth fighting. It meant that you would get up in a meeting and propose a show or a video series, or *Bomb* magazine. You had to argue for your idea and really fight for it because there was not enough money to go around. It was the opposite of I'm okay, you're okay. You had to really stand your ground for what you believed in. I learned to articulate my position there.

SARA: I think people don't realise how prejudiced, sexist they were, even in what you would think is the most enlightened scene.

JANE: A lot of the male members of Colab were like, 'Oh yeah, we love you girls, we should all do this together. And can you, you know, make some copies?' And then when the press would come, they'd be like, 'Don't talk to her, I'll introduce you to the important guys.' A lot of women were also into that. I felt like Jean-Michel at the Times Square show had this whole coterie of the fashion women that were like, 'Oh, yes, Jean, whatever you want, Jean. Can I get you anything else, Jean?' A lot of women wanted to do the mother thing.

SARA: Or they thought that was the role that they were expected to do.

Jane Dickson, *Lolita*, 2020, acrylic on canvas, 165.1 x 185.4 cm
Courtesy of Alison Jacques, London © Jane Dickson; photograph by Paul Hodara

Topless Disco, 2021, oil stick on linen, 121.9 x 76.2 cm
Courtesy of Alison Jacques, London © Jane Dickson; photograph by Paul Hodara

Jane Dickson, *Peepland Angel*, 2017, gouache on tyvek, 45.7 x 60.3 cm
Courtesy of Alison Jacques, London © Jane Dickson; photograph by Michael Brzezinski

I remember some downtown guy filmmaker, when I was producing *Permanent Vacation* for Jim [Jarmusch] in 1979, he said, 'Why don't you just wear your stilettos and forget about making films?' The Whitney is now priding itself on showing a lot of women, finally. June Leaf is now being celebrated, who's been making art for 83 years. I did a retrospective of my films in Madrid and people would ask me, 'Well, why has it been so long between your films?' And I'd say it was a tricky question, because you don't want to come off as a victim. I don't feel like I'm a victim. I know this is the setup. At that time there were only 4% women in television and film in the United States. Now it's 11% so it's getting a little better. But I think people don't realise what we were up against as women in this supposedly outsider scene, that they were treating us in a similar conservative way that the conservative world treated women.

JANE: Just because it's easier to have somebody else clean up and do the errands. Some guys in Colab were really great, like Walter Robinson. He took Yasmin [Ramirez] outside because she was writing art reviews for the *East Village Eye* straight out of high school and Walter said, 'You know, most art critics go to college, and I think I can help you get into Columbia.' And he got her into Columbia and now she's got a PhD and she's a professor. And Walter curated a show at Artists Space very early on of the Colab girls because after the Times Square show all the guys got offers from dealers and not the women. So he did a show of me and Kiki and Becky Howland, and Cara Perlman, and maybe Christy Rupp. It was a step, but these days I don't want to do women shows.

SARA: That's a ghettoisation. I hate that, I don't do women film festivals.

JANE: Having the same reproductive parts doesn't mean you have an aesthetic connection. It's just a way to go, 'Oh, we've shown 40 women all in one lump show.' At this point in my life, I'm like, either you want to show me because you're interested in what I do, or you're not and that's okay. I think there's a tendency to keep throwing women into the chorus. But it's time for me to do my solo, my aria. Back then I do feel like I just was fucking persistent. I couldn't stop. I really do think that's the definition of an artist – somebody that can't help it. And some of us can funnel our compulsions into something that the rest of the world finds interesting. I'm excited to get to know people that are really doing things. I gave an art school talk a while ago and at the end, somebody put up their hand to ask 'How do you get to know famous people?' None of my friends were famous when I met them. They were just imaginative and energetic. Colab artists would ask, 'Why do you have all these different friends from outside our group?' I love many of them but I feel like I was forever squished into a sort of junior member role in that group. There were other places where I got to breathe more. I was friends with the Just Above Midtown people, like David Hammons and Janet Henry. There's a show at MoMA now. I worked for Janet teaching an animation class in Jamaica Queens when I first came to New York and she took me to Just Above Midtown and I got to be friends with all that group of artists. I've always tried to share opportunities as a way to stimulate ideas. For the Times Square show, I persuaded my boss at the lightboard to let me make an ad for the show. It was literally around the corner from the Times Square show. I was programming the sign so I ran the ad every 20 minutes for a month. And through that I got to be friends with Jenny Dixon who was running the Public Art Fund and we started 'Messages to the Public', the first digital artists public series that continues to this day in a different form. For the first year, I said, 'I'll do this for you at the Public Art Fund if I get to be one of the artists in it and I get to pick all the other artists for the first year because I've met all these cool people you never heard of, like Jenny Holzer, Keith Haring, David Hammons, Edgar Heap.' It was a really star-studded list. Barbara Kruger was supposed to participate and so was Nancy Spero, but they got censored because they did pieces about abortion and my boss was Catholic. My impulse wasn't to use my best friends – I'd only just met Keith, he was still at SVA, but I thought his work would translate well to the sign. This was his first public project. Jenny Holzer was printing on paper cups then.

SARA: So where exactly was the sign?

JANE: One Times Square, where the ball drops on New Year's Eve. I ran the ball drop a couple of years, I'd be behind the sign there while doing the countdown. And then in 1982, we had an artist a month, I would help them programme their animation design. I've just been talking to some guy, a curator from the Grand Palais who wants to show them, recreate them in Paris next year, because all I have is a video of them. I saw now that they're doing a thing where you can propose to your sweetheart on Valentine's in Times Square, and that was one of the main money-makers when I first worked there. For $50 you could have a one-minute one-frame thing on the board. And if you wanted a photograph of it, it was $75 – I would go to the other end of 48th street and photograph the sign. It would be like, okay, 7.45 on Friday, you have to put up 'Don, will you marry me?' And it was really fun.

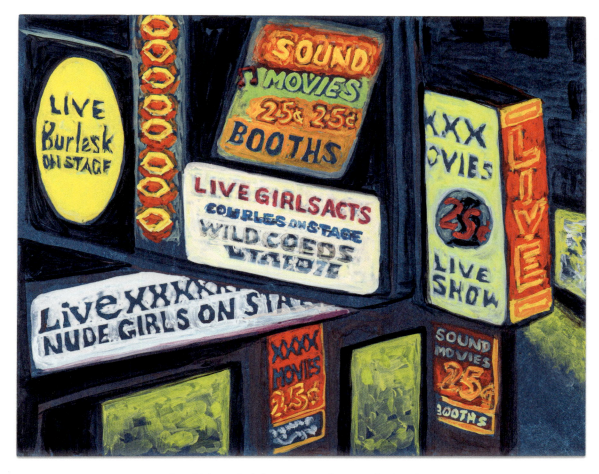

Jane Dickson, *Burlesk 1*, 2017, gouache on tyvek, 48.3 x 61 cm
Courtesy of Alison Jacques, London © Jane Dickson; photograph by Paul Hodara

I would look out the little window behind the sign and I could always figure out who Donna was, jumping up and down in the crowd.

SARA: I wish I'd been there.

JANE: It was really sweet. You know, you could always see who had just been proposed to in the sea of Times Square – the person who's jumping up and down. Different than most of what was going on there.

SARA: That was the foundation of how everything developed from there.

JANE: Once I was working at this lightboard sign, I would rest my eyes periodically from the computer screen by looking out the window when I was taking a break. I'd be like, 'Whoa, oh, my God, oh, look at that.' And I thought, I want to document my time and my place. And right now, this is my time and my place. I think it was Baudelaire who said the artist should be a witness of his time. And I thought, 'Yes, I'm going to take that literally.' That's why I did that little book *Hey Honey Wanna Lift?*. Because those were the pickup lines I was getting when I was applying for jobs in the 70s and going to clubs. During that whole period the Times Square redevelopment project was already in place. Sixth Avenue had already been transformed into modern high rises in the late 60s, I think, or early 70s. Seventh Avenue and Eighth Avenue were frozen, they looked like Hopper paintings, because all the buildings were from the 30s and 40s. Nothing was being changed or improved, pending the city demolition. That's why we could afford this loft there. It was cheap because the landlord knew that they wouldn't have to evict us, the city, the state was going to evict us. But it also meant that they wouldn't fix anything. I thought, 'This is a weird time capsule that I'm documenting before it disappears. But this is what I see out my window.'

I focus on psychology, on why is that person doing that? I notice things, I notice people doing things that I'm thinking about. When I was first in New York, I now realize I was focusing on being alone at night, because almost all my pictures of that period are of solitary figures in the night. Why the night? Well, I was working the night shift and of course the night is really fraught for women. At that point there were all the Take Back the Night protests, which didn't change much. I thought, Yeah, I'm gonna just act like I'm just one of the guys and I can handle it. But it was scary.

SARA: Yeah, I remember Jim cut my hair so I looked like a boy because I had to go back and forth from film school from Prince Street to Seventh Street at night because I was editing at night. So it was much safer and I learned how to walk like a boy so that I'd look like a boy.

JANE: We were talking about Hopper and I just want to add that I admire him tremendously. I didn't set out to be his echo, he was one of many influences. I believe that each person has certain things that they truly know in their gut that they have to tell, a new angle on something that the rest of us couldn't express. And I remember when I was young somebody asking me what my creative wellspring was. And I blurted out 'fear' and I think that's something I grew up knowing a lot about and wanted to explore...it was necessary for me to keep exploring fear. Times Square at night was a great place for that. People go, 'You know who your work really reminds me of?' Oh my God, not Hopper again! But now I think it's good...he's such an idiosyncratic oddball. And so am I, you know. I loved talking about theory with all my colleagues, peer artists. But the people that I have most gravitated to are not the ones that are following the grad school theory of the moment, they are the oddballs of their own, people like David Wojnarowicz. I was thinking about this recently, because David sought me out. So did David Hammons. I was friends with Jimmy De Sana, he was one of the only other people that lived in Times Square back in the day. And Keith Haring, and I was wondering why I had so many gay guy friends.

SARA: I think that there was a fluidity with sexuality. There was a fluidity with painters being musicians, all this germination that was going on between these different mediums.

JANE: It was a really open time, the powers that be had pretty much written off New York City, and all the powers that be had moved to the suburbs. So their only real experience with the city was taking the train in from Westchester, or Jersey, and they really didn't care what we did.

SARA: Right. One of my favourite graffitis I remember seeing was 'USA out of NYC'.

JANE: I still believe in that one.

SARA: I know, I'm waiting for us to become Luxembourg when we've just separated from the rest of the country and become our own damn rock in the ocean. But let's go on to your most recent work, because you've been looking back a little bit. And tying into the Times Square digital lightboard, that must have had an effect on you using astroturf, on using different textures to paint on.

JANE: The lightboard totally made me obsess on signs and light out of the darkness, because that was the world that I was working in. And to this day, I'm pondering what it means to display a sign that says 'Do not follow'. I'm not interested in photo realism – photo realists often focus on the visual effects of bland signs. I'm interested in the psychology of signs that

Jane Dickson, *Temporary Tattoos*, 2005, oil stick on linen, 188 x 137.2 cm
Courtesy of Alison Jacques, London © Jane Dickson; photograph by Deedee deGelia

give you insights into what our culture is desiring, because advertising is all about tantalizing us with things that advertisers know we want. I woke up last night and suddenly thought, I need to do a painting or series of paintings called *Paradise*. I haven't started it yet. But at the moment, I want paradise.
SARA: What does paradise mean to you?
JANE: In light of my current challenges, it's a moment to be striving for the unreachable, you know, imaginary perfection. I don't have an image of a sign that says 'Paradise'; I did just do one that says 'Promised Land'. It's a housing development in this neighbourhood and we were just driving by and I took a picture of it. It says 'Promised Land, all cash'. And it's a really shitty building. Over there, there's one that says 'Dreams Adult Bar', this guy walking around with a sandwich board that says 'Dreams'. I'm like, 'Yeah, we all have dreams. Can I follow you and get to my dreams?' I feel like the thing all my work has in common, whether it's casinos or Coney Island, it's tinsel and crap, you're going to win some fuzzy piece of junk that you could buy for less than you've just paid for the tokens to try to win it. But there's a primal thing in wanting to win something. So it's all about aspiration, and the gap between aspiration and fulfilment. And somehow that's my world.
SARA: I thought I read somewhere that you were influenced by the Japanese painter Hokusai and, you said, [photographer] Weegee.
JANE: I love Weegee, and [American photographer] Diane Arbus. And Weegee lived on 8th or 9th Avenue, not far from where I lived...I think his widow was still alive and I'm sorry that I didn't go introduce myself to meet her. When I decided to paint Times Square – and this is a really early one, *Paradise Alley*, it's on textured vinyl wallcovering – I thought, how can I do these, these city scenes are like canyons. The same way that the Chinese and Japanese make vertical landscapes where you're looking down steep mountains, I thought, that's a good format for cityscapes. So 90% of my early ones are the format and size of a door or window. They're tall and skinny, which is sort of the opposite of the Western landscape tradition. When I was in college I was a night watchman at the Fogg Museum and I would hang out in the Asian rooms in the middle of the night.
SARA: You've been to Asia a few times now, to China, to South Korea, with your work. And has that had any influence on your new work at all?
JANE: I'm fascinated by it. I think, ready or not, this is the Asian century. It's not the European or the American century. I think Korea seems amazing. China, Korea, Japan – they all have such long cultural histories and deeply refined aesthetic traditions to learn from. I'm in an exhibition now at the UCCA museum in Beijing and I'm going to be in the Hong Kong Frieze art fair. I've gone to Asia multiple times. I went to China three times on academic junkets with the Confucius Institute, which is the Chinese government programme that aims to get everyone to speak Chinese because it's their century. They're right. And if you took some Chinese lessons, they would bring you to China. I spent time in Nanjing, Shanghai, Beijing and Xinjiang, the desert at the far end of the Silk Road. That was amazing. It's now closed to Westerners.
SARA: It fascinates me...if you go to the Met, and you see Asian scrolls from 800 or 900 AD, they're so sophisticated with how they see perspective. And then you look at the Mediaeval manuscripts and they're so flat, they have no sense of perspective at all. So, art and Asian art and Western thought process, it's interesting.
JANE: You know, I also went to Japan on the Wild Style tour – it was such a culture clash, it was mind-boggling. I've now been to Japan three times. You can't see your own culture if that's the only culture you live and breathe, you're inside it. Watching television in Japan, I somehow thought they were much more sexually conservative than we are. But then they have dancing underpants crotch shots in an ad for toilet paper or something. That would never happen in America. So it's just that the lines are cut and zigzagging all different ways of what's proper and acceptable. And it's like, Whoa, that's out of bounds. I love to travel to just go, Whoa, that's unexpected.

Growing up spending a lot of time in France, I felt I was always going to be an outsider. Even my British father's parents thought of us as their American grandchildren. Like, we were foreign to them. I thought, if I'm American and I can't blend in here, even with my family, I better figure out what American is, what is different about me and my expectations. I've made my job examining pieces of America, to tease out our hopes and dreams. What are our signs, what are people doing on the street? To clarify our options and our choices.
SARA: Have you ever thought about doing a book of stories to go along with your paintings, because your

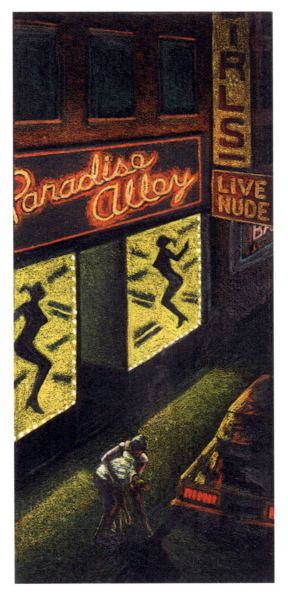

Jane Dickson, *Paradise Alley*, 1983.
Oil stick on canvas, 228.6 x 101.6 cm
Courtesy of Alison Jacques, London © Jane Dickson; photograph by Paul Hodara

paintings are like little movies. You almost want to know what's going on outside the frames.
JANE: It's a good idea and a publisher suggested that to me, but I just haven't done it. About six or seven years ago, Johan Kugelberg founder of Boo-Hooray [an organisation dedicated to preserving the archives of 20th/21st-century cultural movements] approached me about putting together my archive and selling it to an institution and then doing a book. And because of that, I had to go through all those dusty drawers that I hadn't looked at in decades, and then put the images together. And that prompted a period of retrospection, review, where I had to look at what I had done. And I thought, if I was going to leave this now, given that this is what I have, what do I wish I had done that could be the in-betweens, things that are waiting to be done. I think that was partly inspired by seeing the [American painter] Stuart Davis show at the Whitney. He was somebody who did okay paintings in Paris as a young man, little cubist-inspired paintings. And then he came back to America and I think he worked in advertising. And he re-addressed all his early work and did it in this flat, collage, advertising style – they're very American, and bigger than these moody little cubist paintings that he had done that were meaningful to him, but not to the rest of the world. This later work was fabulous. And I thought, given that this is what I've done, what's missing, what things are still waiting to be done? I've had a lot of health issues throughout my adult life. There have been a number of periods when I was rolling on something, but then I had an operation and didn't do anything for a while. And by the time I was better, I was thinking about something else. So I felt like every body of work had gaps. During the pandemic, Johan loaned me his Hasselblad scanner, because when we did my book we only used slides. My assistant needed work, so I said, 'Here's the scanner, here's shopping bags full of scratched-up dirty negatives – please wipe them off and scan them.' I had hundreds of images of Times Square in the 80s that I really hadn't looked at since. And now with Photoshop, you can lighten up the underexposed ones and find lost corners of that time. They're pretty grainy, so you wouldn't want to show prints of them, but they're fine to make paintings from. I felt like I had opened up this peep hole into my past.
SARA: So these new paintings address old subjects? I found a bunch of old slides of mine, but they've decayed. So I have this fantasy of putting them in a projector and then painting the decayed slides – where you can just see a little bit of a person's head. They're just so spooky and strange.
JANE: At least scan them so they get frozen where they are now. I'm really happy that we've scanned.
SARA: So do you mainly use oil stick?
JANE: I use oil stick and acrylic. I used to use oil paint, but after I was sick I stopped using it. In the last five years, I've been trying to wean myself off oil and learn to love acrylic. These two are oil on astroturf, which doesn't really make sense. But I was using oil paint on canvas so I thought, what the hell I'll use it on astroturf now. *Do Not Follow* and *Game* are acrylic on felt.
SARA: Oh, wow, you really don't see the difference – you don't see the difference from the oils!
JANE: I like changing up materials and surfaces because it just freshens it up. And it also pushes my wrist in a different way. So when it gets sore from one thing, I do the other.
SARA: Also, you have to work more quickly with acrylic than with oils?

Jane Dickson, *Winchell's 2*, 2002, oil stick on linen, 81.3 x 132.1 cm
Courtesy of Alison Jacques, London © Jane Dickson; photograph by Paul Hodara

JANE: Yes, it's not a problem because I'm doing these light layers. But I still feel clumsier with acrylic. I totally know what I'm doing with the oil, but with acrylic, the colours don't mix that well. If you get red and white and you mix them, you're not actually gonna get pink, you're gonna get some weird thing. The thing that I did get out of the Punk ethos of the 70s was that I realised that I'm not so interested in materials for their own sake. I thought Eva Hesse was amazing, I loved her work, but I wasn't going to just be about the materials. There's a way that sculpture has explored contemporary materials for the past 100 years; it didn't get stuck in bronze and wax. And painting sort of did get stuck. I thought I could paint on anything. I think partly when I was young, I was intimidated. I thought if I use oil on canvas, I'm getting in the ring with Titian. And I don't know if I want to be compared with Titian. So what if I paint on garbage bags? I painted originally on garbage bags because I wanted a black surface to paint on. It would be like the sign where it was doing lights on darkness. And then I thought about the implications of garbage bags and painting my friends' Punk portraits on garbage bags and conceptually, that is strong. But then I started thinking about it more consciously – I was in Home Depot and I saw these rolls of astroturf hanging down from the ceiling and I'm like, 'Oh my God, it comes in this colour and that colour and I can just ask for 20 yards.'

Also, very early on when I did *City Maze*, a Fashion Moda in 1980, I went to Materials for the Arts, which was brand new at that point. Corporations could give excess materials to the city and they would give them to artists for projects and the companies would get a tax write-off. So I went there and got a couple of rolls of this grey textured vinyl wallcovering. And I went home and started painting on it and I felt like Alice going down the rabbit hole. Because this rough texture breaks up the brushstroke, it makes sort of automatic pointillism. I've also gotten black vinyl and painted on it. I often start series on linen or canvas with a brush until I figure out what the right material is. I have a whole Vegas show that's oil on canvas. But then I realised it should be on felt, like gaming tables. I don't want to start on a neutral ground. I think colour and texture is like key in music. This one for *Fist of Fury* is on this weird green felt which I definitely want to buy more. It's more pea soup colour than pool table but you know these companies come and go and the quality changes and that's somewhat interesting for me to experiment with. And those are oil stick on black gesso. Now you can buy black gesso – when I started doing those it didn't exist.

SARA: You know I love your use of light and shadow and I think the reason I'm so drawn to your work is that it comes from the darkness. Something I've always loved about film, too, is this idea that if you dimly light something, audiences just get upset, they get psychologically disturbed. And it could be a very friendly thing going on. But if it's darkly, dimly lit, it plays on people's psyche.

JANE: I'm a cinematic groupie.

SARA: I can tell. Your paintings have a lot of movement in them.

JANE: I watched a lot of film noir as a kid. It was a big plus when I realised as a young painter of Times Square, that I could put light wherever I want you to pay attention, and whatever I don't care about it's going to disappear into the shadow. Which is the difference between me and the photo realists who always have bright light and they paint absolutely every single thing to the edge of the frame, whether you care about it or not. I set my paintings up, I do a bunch of sketches, and I'm like, 'Where's the action? Where's the light?'

Jane Dickson: Fist of Fury,
11th May–24th June 2023,
at Alison Jacques, 16–18 Berners Street,
London W1T 3LN

Luncheon would like to thank the James Fuentes Gallery

Jane Dickson, *Terminal Bar 2*, 2017, oil stick on linen, 167.6 x 185.4 cm
Courtesy of Alison Jacques, London © Jane Dickson; photograph by Dawn Blackman

Jane Dickson, *Checks Cashed Reflection*, 2022, oil stick on linen, 61 x 81.3 cm
Courtesy of Alison Jacques, London © Jane Dickson; photograph by Paul Hodara

Jane Dickson, *Dobbs Hats*, 1981, acrylic on vinyl, 121.9 x 147.6 cm
Courtesy of the Whitney Museum of American Art, New York; purchased with funds from the Director's Discretionary Fund, David Dickson, and the Boden Kagan Family 2018.66 © Jane Dickson. Image courtesy of the Whitney Museum of American Art, New York; photograph by Deedee Degeli

ALVIN ARMSTRONG

by REGINALD MOORE

Portrait by STORM HARPER

'I'm not a half-stepper,' says Brooklyn-based artist Alvin Armstrong in regards to the comprehensive production of his first monograph Race *(Anna Zorina Gallery Press, 2023). Book aside, that sentiment could just as well apply to Armstrong's approach to the ethics of portraiture. His ability to present the body in leaps and bounds of action is unparalleled. He understands that the purpose of portraiture is not to render the exactness but to justify the essence. If his work appears multi-layered, that is because his brush stroke is heavy and his commitment to the craft is strong. If his work feels inclusive, that is because of what he has learned from listening to Miles Davis – to use 'All Blues.' Alvin Armstrong is not a half-stepper, he is a full-body mover. And you can see it in the work. Our conversation, to coincide with Armstrong's most recent exhibition* Pretty Soon We'll Be Underwater *opening at the Anna Zorina Gallery in Los Angeles, took place on a brisk Saturday morning in March as Armstrong was settling down to work. – Reginald Moore*

Alvin Armstrong: Pretty Soon We'll Be Underwater, 6th May–10th June, at Anna Zorina Gallery, 734 E 3rd Street, Los Angeles
All paintings © Alvin Armstrong/ courtesy of Anna Zorina Gallery.

OPPOSITE: Alvin Armstrong photographed by Storm Harper

Alvin Armstrong, *Out of My Body*, 2022
Acrylic on canvas, 76 x 102 cm

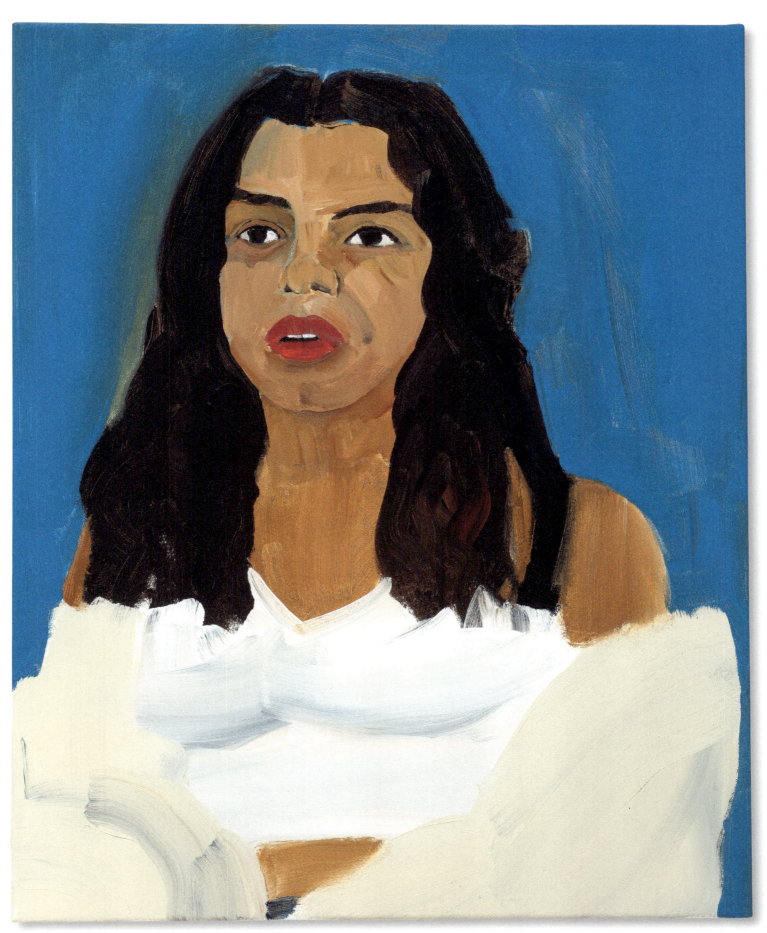

Alvin Armstrong, *Nivia*, 2022
Acrylic on canvas, 56 x 71 cm

Alvin Armstrong, *Tea No Sugar*, 2020
Acrylic on paper, 102 x 163 cm

Alvin Armstrong, *SETH*, 2020
Acrylic on canvas, 56 x 71 cm

REGINALD MOORE: My introduction to your work was the panel of Malcom X portraits, *Malcom Had Feelings Too*. And then I saw a piece of yours in a group show – I can't remember if this show was centred around sports, but I believe it was one of the running paintings. You are a master of stillness and motion. Would you agree with that observation, that you operate between stillness and motion in your paintings?

ALVIN ARMSTRONG: You know I appreciate that observation...what I'll say first is I would pretty much agree with it. In the stillness paintings, I try to create motion in the technique and rhythm and pace that I paint. So if someone's looking at an image where the figure might be sitting, they can still, if nothing else, *feel* a movement in it. I'm always trying to expand what I can do with the paint, but I think that's fair to say.

REGINALD: What about working from a photograph as opposed to working from a live model? Does anything get lost in translation when you're working with a prepared image as opposed to person-to-person contact?

ALVIN: Definitely, that's a great question. You know my favourite way to paint is with live subjects. It's what I describe as my graffiti if you will. A freedom to just feel it out and let things flow. So much is lost looking at still imagery, it's a completely different process. What you do with that imagery and how you enhance what you're looking at, or what you pull from things, that's a beauty in itself. But it's a completely different feeling, process, technique and so forth. I think that there are people that do that extremely well and then there's others that do other things very well. For me, I don't want to just do the live portraits so I like to challenge myself to do both. From the beginning, I challenged myself to practise both skills so that as my practice grew, I could have different avenues of creativity to go down. If I got bored with one way that I work, I could always invite someone in to paint live. Painting is so isolating and it's a blessing to be able to call friends and people that I admire, influences in to sit for me. It's for the most part a very casual experience that I've worked hard at in order to gain the skills necessary to have it be so. I'm never trying to paint the spitting image of what's in front of me, it's more about the sharing of energies between the two people and my interpretation of the mood and sensibilities. The times it's not successful I feel like I get off that centre, I worry too much about one thing or I'm too literal with it.

REGINALD: What did you do during the pandemic when you weren't able to have person-to-person contact?

ALVIN: My first show was September 2020, so I literally arrived on the scene in the pandemic. I had started painting two years before that and what the live portraiture looked like in the beginning was my good friends and the few people I was around, self-portraits. But it was a painful process at first. What took me three, four hours in the beginning now doesn't take nearly the same amount of time. When we were in lockdown I wasn't doing live portraits. My work was mostly responding to the trauma that was happening and the Black lives lost leading up to that first show with the Malcolms. For the majority of the time, if it's not moving me internally – be it a relationship, something I see, hear or read about – it's not really for me. I'm really trying to move myself in the process, but also impact others that see the work.

REGINALD: Is there something in painting that you can do now after years of commitment to your craft, that you were unable to do, say, five years ago? I was listening to a podcast and another artist was talking about how she can't paint or draw shoes. She said after years of trying she still cannot do it. Is there something similar to that that you can either still not do or you've mastered? Does that question make sense?

ALVIN: I don't know how much you know of my story, but I've only been painting for a little over four and a half years, so it's all new to me. But I'm obsessed and in that time, I've painted quite a bunch. Two weeks in, I didn't even attempt to paint faces, I always wanted to approach learning in an organic way. So, once I started painting figures, which was pretty quickly, my first painting was a self-portrait. Once I started to dive in and figure things out more, I started painting silhouettes of friends – I would just paint their clothes and a blank face... more simplistic portraits if you will. I still have those. As I gained skill and technique, I slowly began to add more of the full picture. What's interesting is now, after four and a half years of obsession, I'm actually beginning to turn around from being focussed on proportion and how things look correctly. I'm really starting to bend and expand what a hand can be or how much I can take away. It's really been quite a journey but I'm in a place right now that's really fun. It's fun to extend an arm to be bigger than another, but I didn't want to jump ahead to that place before I really understood what I was doing. So, I took a real methodical approach to gaining the skill to paint the whole figure. I would say hands probably came last, hands and feet if I'm being honest, and I too did the same thing – before I even dove into extremities, I just cropped figures and zoomed in on them enough to where they didn't fit in the frame anyway. But it didn't feel forced, I just made sure that the figure was big enough that it obviously went beyond the frame, and I think a lot of people recognise my paintings with crops in them and I still crop to this day. A lot of the time I'll crop the head just a bit or part of the body some – I like the crop feel, but again, my practice is always evolving and it's what I love about it. I like to keep the challenge fresh so even that's changing. I'm starting to shrink the figure and I'm starting to bring in other pieces – in my studio, when someone's sitting, I'm starting to paint the hardwood floors into the painting. Like earlier in my path, I'm slowly and organically bringing in things but I still think, with my practice, it's more about what isn't there than what is – than to paint everything that I see like my desk, a bottle and a cup. I don't really have interest painting things just because they're there.

REGINALD: As an artist, are you always thinking in or of colours? You know how musicians talk about being keen to sound, is there a particular colour that you are drawn to?

ALVIN: I really just trained my eye to what I liked. It's been trial and error so much, that I think subconsciously I've gotten familiar with colour combinations and, if I'm using a lot of blues, what feels right to go with those blues. It's not something that I overthink, I try to keep it close to my heart and what feels right. I would say that over 90 per cent of the time, the colours that I've chosen remain the colours...I'm not one to second guess my choices with colours. Now the way that that's changed is I used to blow through paintings – at the time I started painting, I would have obsessed so much about what I think I wanted to do or what not, that once I got going I blew through it. Now what I'm doing in my studio is I'm sitting with the paintings more. I'll paint some of the figure and I'll sit and look at it for a couple of days, add a few things, take away a few things. With that comes a different colour story, a different rhythm with how I go about choosing the overall composition of colour. It's challenging to keep it fresh and not get bored. I think I have a palette that I'm familiar with but I also like switching it up. More than anything, I try to give myself room to evolve as much as possible and not limit myself to what I'm familiar with.

REGINALD: When you are in working mode, what is a typical day in the studio like for Alvin Armstrong?

ALVIN: From the beginning, my style has always been that I'm up with the sun and my work stops basically at sun down. For me the most creative, impactful space within a day is sunrise and quickly thereafter. So I'm in here early, no one's in the building – there's probably about twenty other studios in here and no one's here when I am here. The space is pretty much clean when I get here because when I leave the day before, I make sure I break down in a certain way so when I re-enter the next morning, it feels good. I have the air purifier, I turn that on at night just to clear the energy. I get in here, I light some Palo Santos and I pick a record... I only play original vinyl records.

REGINALD: That was going to be the next question, music!

ALVIN: Music is a huge part of my practice, specifically Bebop jazz. The playlist is pretty boring because I stay with the greats. I always wonder if anyone has played *Kind of Blue* more than me since I discovered it four or five years ago. It's not the only record I play but I play it a lot. Miles, John Coltrane, Thelonious Monk... I listen to all the greats. When I get in here I turn on a record, I usually already have coffee by then and I just try to clear my head. Sometimes I have a painting that I've already started and I'm getting back into. Wherever I'm at in my process – similar to sports you know – I go through a little warm up. A lot of it is just thought, like placing my heart in the space and clearing my mind, and then I get going. The music really is the catalyst that gets me actually moving the arm and painting. The rhythms really help me get going. Just like going to the gym and working out or sports of any kind, the hardest part of the process is the initiation but once you get your engine going you get lost in what you're doing. There's times when my partner will come and bring me a smoothie or something in the middle of my day unexpectedly, and she'll comment on how I just seem to be in another universe. When I'm not expecting her, I don't have that transition – like, oh I'm going to see somebody – so she can really get a sense that I'm in another place. It's so intense – I try to explain this a lot to people – that it's both relaxing and intense. When I'm painting a portrait, it's casual, but the focus on what's actually taking place is so intense. I do it so much that it may come off as casual, light, but the focus required is intense.

REGINALD: You can see in the work that it's serious. When you were talking earlier, you said that when you first started you didn't really do faces. I think faceless art is so interesting because it allows the viewer to step into the work...it becomes a portrait of the viewer. I like what you said about music; about there being a type of music or a particular musician that gets the mind prepared and keeps the hand moving...

ALVIN: ...because that's exactly what it is. I call my painting rhythm paintings...there is so much that happens in the process and it's why I move the way I do. That's not my creation, I learn from my heroes Miles Davis, Bob Marley, Nipsey Hussle – these are my heroes in terms of their verve for life, in how they lived, so I really hold onto the fact that my paintings, more than anything else, are rhythm paintings. I turn on the engine and I've got to get that rhythm, or it doesn't really work. If I get off track, the public's not going to see that painting because I'm not going to like it as much. How you described being able to dive into the painting, even though you're not there, I really intentionally try. I think that's what's created with keeping the pace up to a certain degree – you can tell a hand made this, it's not a picture, it's very different. I love photography but with a painting, I always want it to be a little off. I want you to see drips a little bit if they happen – if they don't, they don't. I want it to feel as organic and alive as possible, being that it's flat. Another thing about my work is that the texture of the painting is so important – it's what the viewer misses online and hopefully it's a pleasant surprise when you see it in person and you almost want to touch it. I *love* texture, I *love* going over old paintings, I *love* bringing out different levels and surfaces because I don't want it to be just a clean pretty thing. That's not what I'm trying to do. I want to tug at your heart; even when someone's still, I want to tug at the heart, man. If it's history, it's reminding you of something, I'm aiming at your heart. The more I paint, the less I'm connected to over-explaining specific pieces to people, because I really want someone to have their own experience with it. If someone asks specifically how I feel about something, I'll let them know, but really I want people to have their own experience with it.

REGINALD: You know we were talking about connecting with history and about stepping into the paintings? Those running paintings made me think of my grandfather. My grandfather's claim to fame was that he ran against Jesse Owens. He would tell that story, and every time he told it he changed his ranking from second place to third place. Nobody in the family even knows if the story was true [*laughs*]. When I saw that painting I thought, there's my grandfather running against Jesse Owens.

ALVIN: Do you have photos of that?

REGINALD: No, nobody does. It was just this story that he told everyone about Jesse Owens and him…

ALVIN: That's amazing, I appreciate you sharing that with me. That was at my solo show two years ago, at Anna Zorina I'm pretty sure…two runners? With the runners, it's the movement but it's also everything that goes into it, the emotion. I'll always paint Black runners… it symbolises so much – we'll never stop running in this country, whether it's towards something or away from something. I just love the symbolism in it and also, wrapped up in that, the '96 Olympics with all those heroes of mine – Micheal Johnson, Carl Lewis, Jackie Joyner. All those heroes… especially at that time during my adolescence…they just did so much for my spirit. So that will continue to be weaved into what I do. I love painting heroes of mine.

REGINALD: You know you touched on how you love photography? I have a tendency to couple the arts. Like when I think of photography, I attach prose to it. When I think of painting, it's like film is involved – I think it may be because it's a frame and you're surrendering into it. The story is in front of you, but you must be willing to step into it. I know it's usually the opposite for some people, because books are often illustrated. But when I think of painting and art, there's a film element at work for me. Are you inspired by films?

ALVIN: I borrow everything; I don't hold back. For me, the beauty of film specifically is its life – you can hear people, you can feel them, so film is so impactful. In the translation from moving picture to the paintings, there's a bit that gets lost. In terms of what I'm trying to accomplish, there's a little bit of tweaking of composition and what works, but movement of any kind in film always impacts me. I've watched so much live jazz, old films…you can't smell the smoke, but to be able to see the smoke in the room and the tones you get in the browns and the changing of colours in real time – all those things impact what gets translated into the feeling I'm trying to convey in the painting. But that's the practice, that's the skill that I'm really trying to sharpen in here every day – how do I translate whatever I'm in front of, whatever I see. Henry Taylor is my art hero (I say this all the time). I think he's a genius at what he does, and he does it better than anyone else and that is his reinterpretation. Henry can take the most iconic photograph of the most famous people and the shapes are the same but it's very much his own. When he's done with that painting, he's translated it in a way where you can very easily find the photograph he used, but his interpretation is so honestly pure and it works. It's respected and no one second guesses his source, or at least it doesn't matter because he's so honest and authentic in his approach and that skill is so rare. I'm working on my ability to do that in my own way.

REGINALD: Well, I think you're already there.

ALVIN: I appreciate that.

REGINALD: I can automatically spot an Alvin Armstrong painting, and I can tell when somebody else has looked at an Alvin Armstrong painting. But you are right, Henry Taylor is a genius. But the styles are so different…his paintings to me are very particular, like *Cicely and Miles Visit the Obamas*. Just like you said, when you go back and you visit that original photograph, it's like you have to know something about putting paint on canvas to come up with that effect.

ALVIN: That's one of my favourite paintings. I think it's the hand, where the hand is in the picture…that's definitely the source but it's so authentically his, and what he chooses to extract and leave is just amazing.

REGINALD: Okay, I have one last question for you about your recent book. I love the title *Race*. I'm guessing it's a double entendre.

ALVIN: It totally is…

REGINALD: You know the reason I connected with the art in this volume is because my family used to go to the Kentucky Derby and the horse races. Somewhere there's a pictures of them all dressed up at the races. I was so thrilled to have this book, and I'm so glad you came out the gate with a strong monograph. So, talk to me about putting this together.

ALVIN: First of all, thank you so much…I was going to ask you about it, because I know how near and dear books are to you, I respect what books are to you, I respect your eye for quality and presentation and feel. It makes so, so happy that you responded in the way you did, because we spent about a year on that thing, and the reason being is I didn't want to come out with any book if I wasn't going to be extremely proud of it. That book is in chronological order of those paintings…there's thirty-five in total. From the first one to the last one, that's the order that I painted them over the course of 2021. The special thing about that book is as you go from painting to painting, you can literally see my process shift with my familiarity with subject and location painted. Halfway in, at twenty, I got my first studio – I used to paint out of my apartment – and even that shift totally influenced the paintings and they started getting way looser. I just breathed more in my space, and it's reflected in the paintings. It's so special to me and of course Larry Ossei-Mensah helped me with the interview, and you know I respect him so much and his hard work in the industry. We got another writer – Amber Officer-Narvasa – and she talks about horse racing and so forth…she gave me one of my first show reviews for the first show with the Malcolms in it. The process took some time, but Anna Zorina and her whole team support me so whole-heartedly and are so patient and I just appreciate them so much. When I started making that series and I got to about ten, I knew that I wanted to do something else with the series besides just show them so I mentioned that maybe I want to do a book with this and from that day forward she was just so supportive in making it happen. At certain parts of the process, I was second guessing – oh, maybe we shouldn't – but she really stuck by me and pushed me to do it and I could not be happier. There's not one thing I would change about how that book came out. I was worried about the colours because I didn't understand the process of taking a painting and then colourising it. It's not just a case of taking a photo and then printing it – they have to recreate the colours with the technology used. It can be a challenging process at times but I could not be happier.

REGINALD: It even smells like paint.

ALVIN: That's amazing, that makes me feel so good. My mum's dad, my grandpa, had a ranch in Arizona so twice a year we would go there and we would ride the horses like it was nothing. For me, that whole series is just like a nostalgia on that time and adds to the narrative of who's on horses. I'm super-proud of the work and I really appreciate your words with that.

REGINALD: Even the size of the book… It's so important to have a beautiful first book.

ALVIN: I'm not a half-stepper – you know what I mean? The paintings are an awkward, large, long size so right away we wanted to make sure that the dimensions matched the paintings.

REGINALD: Well, I appreciate you taking the time to talk to me and sharing your insights on your work.

ALVIN: The feeling's mutual. You know I've watched what you do from afar and I hope this is the beginning of a friendship – I mean that wholeheartedly. If you're ever in New York please come by and sit for me… I'd love to get you memorialised. Just keep doing you and staying authentic to who you are and don't let anyone tell you otherwise…

REGINALD: I won't. Thank you, I appreciate it.

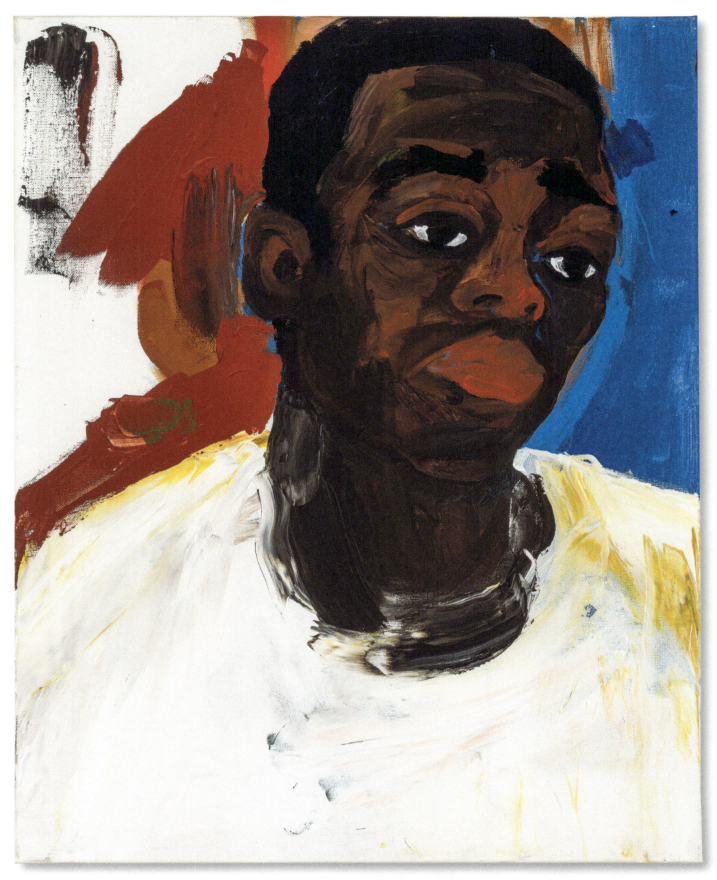

Alvin Armstrong, *Black Thought*, 2020
Acrylic on canvas, 56 x 71 cm

Alvin Armstrong, *Just Like This*, 2022
Acrylic on canvas, 152 x 213 cm

Alvin Armstrong, *Powers That Be*, 2021
Acrylic on canvas, 122 x 183 cm

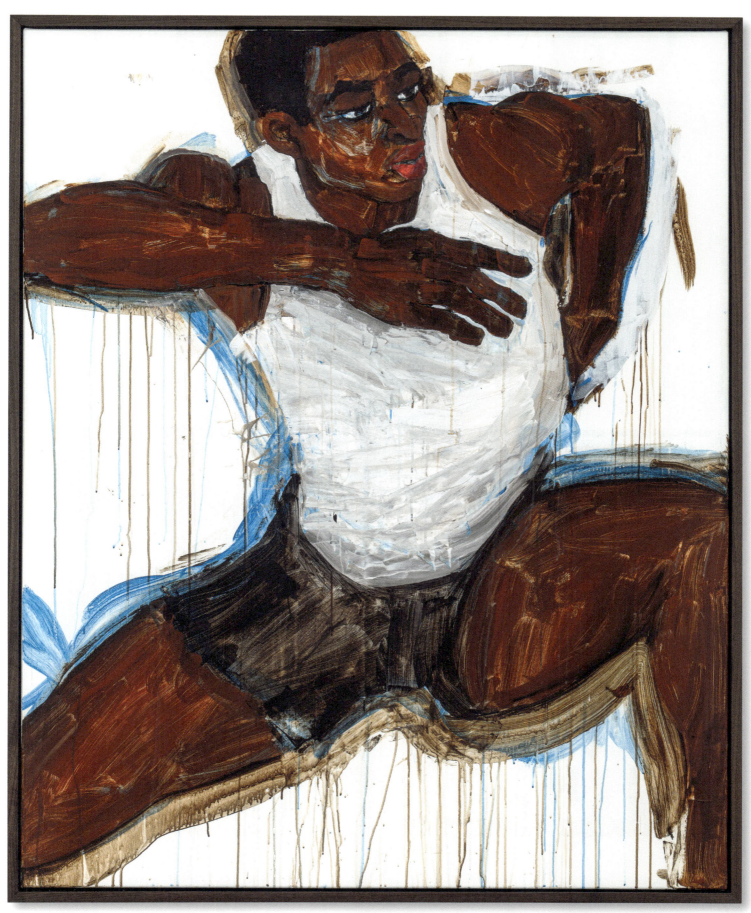

Alvin Armstrong, *Staple*, 2022
Acrylic on canvas, 122 x 175 cm

INSPIRATIONS BY GHETTO GASTRO

Ghetto Gastro Presents Black Power Kitchen
by Jon Gray, Pierre Serrao, Lester Walker with Osayi Endolyn. Artisan Books © 2022

Ghetto Gastro was founded as a culinary collective by trio Jon Gray, Pierre Serrao and Lester Walker in 2012. From its Bronx roots it has a global reach across the disciplines of art, fashion and food. Across these pages the squad selects some of the artworks, people and images that have fed the inspiration behind their work and discuss with their friend Nell Kalonji, fashion editor and stylist, the histories and meetings that drive them forward.

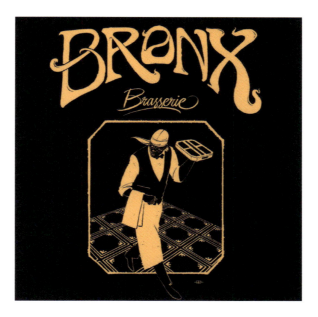

Illustration by Wu Yué for Ghetto Gastro's pop-up Bronx Brasserie, created in partnership with Cartier at Place Vendôme, Paris in 2021

JON GRAY: I woke up and realised I had no food, so I got to go get me some lunch [in the car]. It's on brand because it's *Luncheon* magazine...

FRANCES ARMSTRONG JONES: We've never had an in-motion lunch like this before...without the lunch!

NELL KALONJI: Thank you for doing this. As a number one Ghetto Gastro fan, I'm so excited that this is finally working out. I wanted to start with a little bit about how we met six, seven years ago now.

JON: That sounds right. Everything before covid is blurry on the time line...but I know it was a long time ago.

NELL: I don't even know how...I think it must have been online somehow that I came across you guys. We did this section for the magazine at the time – it was basically inviting people that are interesting to your dinner party and I was really drawn to Ghetto Gastro. I fell into one of those real deep research holes and I was like, Okay I've got to meet these guys somehow. I think what really drew me to you was that you don't have an approach to food in the regular sense, in what you expect a chef to talk about and do in their life. It's really a three-hundred-and-sixty-degree approach, an approach that gives back with pride in its heritage, but also highlights what food means in a social circumstance and in a political sense, especially for the Brown and Black community in America and the world in general and how this plays into race and society and class. I thought that was really interesting. I think the sky is the limit; anything you told me that you were doing, I wouldn't be surprised. It would be really interesting for us to know how it all came about.

JON: Just to tap in on how we first met, you put us in those Craig Green cloaks – we called that our *Game of Thrones* shoot.

NELL: Oh my god! I love that. It was in some small apartment somewhere in Midtown, New York.

JON: It was so dope, with crazy curtains and that shit... I think we collect people along the journey, so that's why we feel blessed to have you as part of our family. The GG thing started in the Bronx – Lester and I grew up in the same neighbourhood in Co-op City, Section 5, and my grandmother was actually his younger brother's teacher. His younger brother and I were really close in my earlier years, he was someone I looked up to, like a big brother figure to me. So our families were always connected and then I knew Lester as a chef because he was going to a school called Park West, which is now called Food and Finance. They have culinary programs for high-school students and one of my friends from my building was also on the program. I had always loved food, never thought it would be a vocation, but just loved it as a passion. We always bonded and linked up in that shared passion, but Ghetto Gastro came about after my fashion. I had a T-shirt start up and a denim line but I was burned out because it wasn't going how I wanted it to go. I was like, Man what would I be doing if it wasn't for the money? Because I was doing fashion for the money. I like getting fly and fresh and all that shit, but I was chasing the bag and also just trying to stay out of jail, because I had a court case. When I really thought about, when I did the soul-searching and thought about what I would do if it was purely based on my desires, I thought it would be something that was centred on food and travel. With Ghetto Gastro, it's just an expression of us taking the power back. Coming from the Bronx, probably still the poorest borough in New York City, we felt like we've been contributing on the global stage of culture in a major way, but not capturing any of that value. So Ghetto Gastro was like a celebration of the culture – Black culture – and of being from the Bronx. It's about capturing value, reclamation, through our creative output and using food as a medium because as humans, everybody has to eat right? It's one of the things we all do. We really wanted to centre the stories on the people that are responsible for making it. Think about American food, it's largely rooted in Black food or Native American food, so those are the vibes. That was the start and the political, radical aspect of it is just because those are the households we grew up in. Some of my first reading material was the autobiography of Malcom X – my mum's just giving me these books at a young age so they became some of the foundation. But I understand everybody doesn't have the same opportunity – there's structures and systems in place that have been oppressing communities for hundreds of years.

NELL: I remember during the pandemic when you guys did food carts and those T-shirts. I think I saw something that you posted about how food is power and how that can be misused, and how people can be suppressed through that because it's something that, as you said, everyone needs.

JON: Exactly, that graphic was 'Food is a Weapon' designed by New Studio. I'm sure the same goes in London – certain people have less access to the delicious nutritious option and covid really exacerbated that. Just seeing how that related to the poor health outcomes; these things aren't a mistake. The US government subsidises people that farm corn and soy, but the corn is not always even for food but for fuel. So they get government credits for this, but nothing for growing leafy greens and those types of things that are more nutritious and perishable. So these structural things lead to certain outcomes like the access to information and access to the actual product, so food can be used as a tool to oppress people. I feel like our liberation is in the soil as well, so food can also be a weapon of class destruction – Lester coined that phrase, that's his quote. So we look at it both ways – it's been used as a tool for negative, but we want to reverse its narrative and use it as a tool for positive.

NELL: Before we jump into your visual references, since I've known you, I've realised pretty quickly that all of you guys, but you specifically, are very visual. I think everything with Ghetto Gastro in general is very visual, even your cookbook. The photography is community based and visual. There's three of you, so then when did Pierre come into the equation?

JON: I was living in Long Island City, I had an apartment there, and we were doing a lot of GG parties at the apartment. I was at the gym working out with my boy Chike (of the direction and production film-making duo Coodie and Chike – they actually did the Kanye documentary *Jeen-Yuhs*). We were working out and P [Pierre Serrao] was in there with a group of fellas working out and I overheard them talking about the tuna tartare at this restaurant called Morimoto. It's funny but I was at this restaurant the day before. It was acclaimed and fancy and, especially back then, there weren't a lot of people of colour dining there. So when I heard him talking about Morimoto's tuna tartare I was surprised because typically that's not what people were discussing when they were lifting weights. It intrigued me to see a young Black man discussing that, so I asked him what he was in to and he said he's a chef and I was like, Ah alright, I work in food too. I started this collective and he joined two years after we started but we met early on and me and him just became super cool. You know how we do it, we collect friends. He lived across the street and whenever my girlfriend at the time would get mad at me, I would call him up and be like, 'Bring us some weed or something man, she's bugging out, we got to chill her out.' So that was how we got super close and then we did a party for *Playboy* on my terrace and he brought some salads and some dishes that people loved and I was like, 'Alright man, you're initiated into the gang.'

NELL: Okay, so we asked you guys to curate this section. Let's go through the images and you can tell me why they are important, how you came across them and why they are meaningful to you. What about the Bronx Brasserie illustration?

JON: That's an image that our homie Wu Yué, our Chinese brother from Paris, illustrated. We did a project with Cartier and took over the Place Vendôme. We had one side of the square as a traditional French bistro and the other side felt a little more contemporary, you know bling-bling. He drew the dude in the bistro with a durag because we practice Durag Diplomacy, so that was on the menu. I just really loved this image and the nature of the collaboration because he was able to whip this up fairly quickly. It was really dope, doper than I could have expected it to be from the commission. It was a lot of fun. We had our friends at Nuovo Design make these crazy rectangular Marsotto marble lunch trays in the shape of Place Vendôme with bevelled edges. It was referencing prison...like subversive text you know? The school to prison pipeline, because you have lunch trays in school, but then they also have lunch trays in prison. And because we carved it in marble, it was very heavy so it was just like subversive sneak attack knowledge. The people that were eating had no idea that's what it meant, but we knew...

Ghetto Gastro Ogún chef knife crafted in collaboration with Sakai Takayuki and Yanagi Knife. Yanii Gough photographed by Bobby Rogers

NELL: I saw that…wish I could have been there. Okay, next we have an image of a woman holding a knife to her hair.

JON: Yanii Gough, the model we shot is from the Bronx, she's super dope. This is a knife we had made. We designed it and created it and it was really about celebrating cultural collision and especially telling stories that centre on what people might consider the global south, looking at Afro-Asiatic storytelling. Thinking about the Yoruba Orishas and the travel of Africans and the culture, how it would boomerang from West Africa and came to the Americas through the trading and the movement of people. So this blade is called Ogún, which is an orisha of iron, technology and war in the Yoruba religious tradition. And then you had Shogun, which is the Japanese period of the Samurai and knife-makers usually descended from sword-makers. We wanted to honour Yasuke, the Black samurai. So all this storytelling we did around the release of this limited-edition blade. I really love this image – Yanii actually has a cut on her face, that [actual] scar is from a knife. Bronx shit.

NELL: So this image was specifically created for your knife release? It's beautiful. This is why I wanted to work with Ghetto Gastro on this. There are always layers to everything you do – an intentional meaning. Sometimes the meaning is simply to bring the community together but often it goes even deeper.

OPPOSITE AND ABOVE: Photographs by Joshua Woods

NELL: Anyway, the next image is a sunset.
JON: That might be a sunrise or a sunset, I'm not sure…that's the neighbourhood me and Lester grew up in. The building on the right is Lester's building. The picture is taken from my living room – Joshua Woods took it when he was staying with me while we were doing the images for the book [*Black Power Kitchen*, published by Artisan Books, New York, 2022]. So it's just really an homage to our neighbourhood, to the North Bronx, Co-op City.
NELL: So, this is the proximity you grew up in…you could literally see each other.
JON: Yeah, I could throw a rock at his building.
NELL: Next we have a table with some fried food.
JON: Fried calamari, and this spot is called Johnny's Reef on City Island, which if you grew up in the Bronx or in the city, you might know what this is about. It's like a neighbourhood spot and we just vibe out. We call it the 'Hood Hamptons' – if you got a graduation for high school or middle school, or you got a hot date, you're going to City Island. Summertime fine, you feel me?
NELL: I feel you. And is that you in the picture?
JON: That's me, Josh took this picture. He's going to kill me for sending out of focus images to print. Fuck it tho!

Photograph by Joshua Woods

NELL: Then the street signs…it's Jefferson place, Boston Road.
JON: Yeah, Bishop J. Arthur Jones. This is a street named after my great-grandfather, who I'm also named after, in the Bronx. So my name is Jon Arthur Gray, but he's the original Jon Arthur. I wanted to show the people that we're really in these streets for real. He did a lot in the community, so I've always felt that it's a self-imposed burden that I've had. I got big shoes to fill, I got to really represent…
NELL: It's hereditary…
JON: Yeah, I got to do some shit that matters. I'm like, My great-grandfather got a block named after him, I got to do better than him. I'm two generations, three generations removed so it's like a competitive homage, because even when I was in the streets, I always felt really torn because I was part of the destruction of the neighbourhood. I had a lot of conscience because I knew better, but I just chose to do something different because, when you're trying to get to certain places and the options are limited you going to…
NELL: …take the easy road, no?
JON: Nah, it's a hard road, because it's a real decision when you make it. I think my success in the streets gave me confidence to do anything, because I always felt like I had a base level of intelligence or charm or whatever, but it's like I wasn't able to prove that in the typical academic structure. I've dealt with ADHD since I was diagnosed in 8th grade and everything starts to make sense. You start to understand neurology and neuro-diversities. Also, people just typecast young Black boys, it's like we get less chances and less grace when it comes to figuring things out.
NELL: Now though, do you think this is also the roots of Ghetto Gastro? I feel like a lot of people try to leave where they're from behind; in a way, success means that you are growing out of your neighbourhood. Whereas you, you stayed there, and you still live there and you're trying to make it a better place for your community, all of you.
JON: I think a lot of us are told lies. People feel like they have to become something else to reach where they want to go. I think you have to work hard and do things, but this is also the harder road. It would have been easy for me to just be into fashion, changing my actual voice to make certain people feel comfortable. But for me, I think it's more radical to just be who I am and let the work speak.
NELL: I agree, and also what that means for the next generation, for the next young boy.
JON: Exactly, like seeing the reflection. I remember being in school and they'd have the doctors or the lawyers coming and it was like, I don't relate to those people because they're not who I am right now, they weren't the kid who had interest in what I'm interested in at this moment in life. I didn't really see my reflection in those people, so I wanted to make sure that we could be a reflection. We had to create our shit from scratch but not everybody has that confidence or the belief to just do that. Often we need to see things to understand this is how I could do something.

NELL: Next there's a picture of a leaf with a ladybug.
JON: A ladybug is supposed to represent good fortune in many cultures and this was taken in the community garden in the Bronx where Lester has a garden box. Joshua took this photo and for me it's just a subversive way to get red, black and green – African colours – into the spread…community gardens, the Bronx, Black power, all of that.

Photograph by Joshua Woods

Photograph by Joshua Woods

NELL: Okay, then we have a picture of two men in front of two red garage doors.
JON: It's a storage unit. Me and Josh were on the road taking pictures for the book and what not. We were leaving the studio after a food photo and I had to go to the storage unit and there were some West African folks that had a lot of artefacts in the storage facility, different things from West Africa. We pulled up and Josh recognised one of the brothers and he was like, 'Oh yeah, that's my man. It's so crazy because this dude right here is always telling me that he's really tight with Naomi Campbell's people, he's going to get me in touch with Naomi Campbell.' We pull up and Josh says, 'What's up?' and he's like, 'Yo Josh, I got Naomi's friend on the phone.' And it ends up being Desirée, who I know well, who's Naomi's best friend – it's all this crazy connection. But I really like the bridge in the background in the mirror because you can tell he took it from the car. You see the tall buildings, the towers that represent gentrification in the South Bronx behind it? But then you have this West African connection and a personal connection in the photo.

Photograph by Joshua Woods

NELL: Then we have – what are these, African, Egyptian figurines?
JON: These are the orishas that you'd find in the botanica where people that practice Santeria, Ifá amongst other things go. You find a lot of these botanicas in Harlem and in the Bronx wherever you find a lot of Puerto Ricans, Dominicans, Cubans. You have Shango in there and other deities. I just thought it was interesting. Josh took this picture of a window inside a botanica.
NELL: And where was it?
JON: This is in El Barrio in Harlem.
NELL: This was also when you were doing the pictures for the book?
JON: Yup, we're giving you all this exclusive, unreleased material.

Photograph by Joshua Woods

NELL: And next we have an embellished door?
JON: This brings us full circle. This is actually the door to the Supreme Court in the Bronx, which is a beautiful building. But I had to go into the courthouse and a judge told me that I could get ten years to life for my charges. Me and Lester actually reconnected in the courthouse – this was like 2007, 2008 and we hadn't been in touch for a while – so we reconnected, because he had left the neighbourhood. I was still living there but we didn't have each other's cell numbers, but we reconnected in the courthouse. He was leaving probation or something, I was going to court. I told him to come with me to see the judge, because I used to have to go every three months.

NELL: Right. Okay, then we have Sundial, Traditional African Manback.
JON: This is a spot on Boston Road that's known for tonics for health, vitality, and I just always felt like that graphic was super dope. It's just showing this plant-based movement – adaptogenic as they like to call it, like the Goop type of folk. The traditional healthcare system excludes Black folk often, so we'll put together nature's remedies, natural herbs and natural things.

Photograph by Joshua Woods

Photograph by Malcolm McNeil

NELL: And we have a picture of Pierre.
JON: He's getting his hair braided. That's before we did the launch party for our book in the Met, so it's pretty radical to have our collective in this room, the same room where they host the Met Gala. We took over the Temple of Dendur for the party and he had a very Black moment and got his hair braided before the party in the temple, channelling that Beyoncé and Jay-Z apeshit video when they took over the Louvre. We took the temple back to Africa that night, you feel me?

Photograph by Joshua Woods

NELL: And then we have you and Lester and there's some fire going on.
JON: We were in Cognac doing the tour. This is like the younger version of us in 2015, but Pierre just wasn't in this picture. This is where they make the Cognac barrels to age the Cognac.

FOLLOWING SPREAD:
Hugh Hayden, *Soul Food*, 2021, ICA Miami

NELL: So then we have some instruments – saxophones, trumpets…it's Hugh Hayden's *Soul Food*.
JON: Hugh Hayden's a long-time collaborator of ours and he created these brass Jazz kitchen instruments. I think it's a conversation about Black contributions, about how they like to put us in the 'soul' category. Us being Black people that work in food, the first question is, 'Oh is it soul food?' First of all, what does that mean? If you cook with love, you cooking from the soul, so it's like people think all we can do is collard greens and mac and cheese. I just really love this image – we put it in the book, but it's a cropped version.
NELL: Where was it – can you figure out the space?
JON: This is at the ICA Museum in Miami.
NELL: That's actually a real aspect as well. Like Rihanna winning the best urban designer award – as soon as you do a pair of jeans, a tracksuit bottom, then you are a streetwear designer because that is the category that Black designers, female or male, are being put into. It's just the same.
JON: And even the term 'streetwear' is ridiculous, because it's like, Where do people wear clothes? On the streets. Even if you're going to a gala, your foot is going to touch the side walk somewhere. It's just trying to minimise…
NELL: Categorise and minimise.
JON: You know when you go to the classes, they're like, 'Yeah you can make the money.' But that's all – they don't really want to give you full credit.
NELL: No exactly. They put you in a category, your own category.

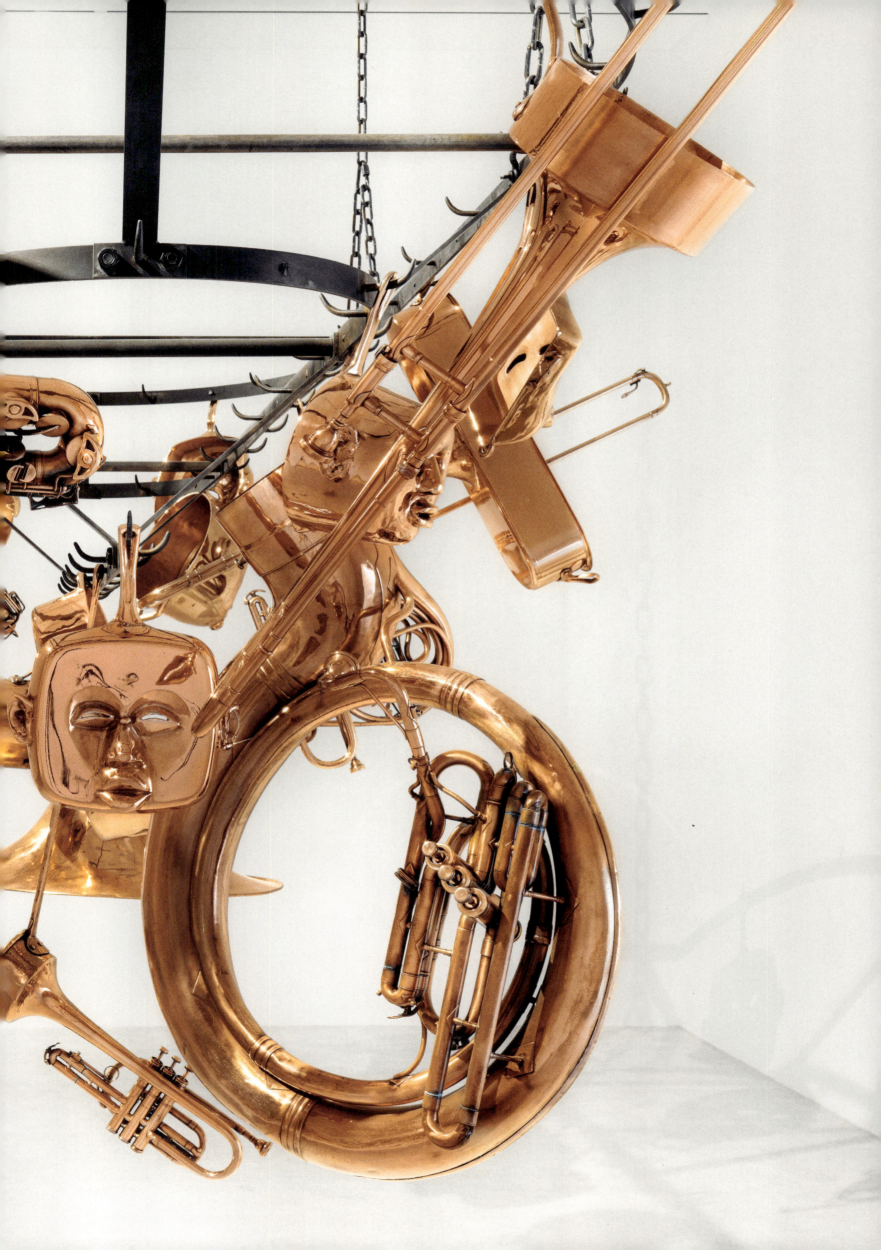

Photograph by Nayquan Shuler for *Ghetto Gastro Presents Black Power Kitchen* by Jon Gray, Pierre Serrao, Lester Walker with Osayi Endolyn. Artisan Books © 2022

NELL: Next there's a sculpture with a…I want to say scoop of ice cream?
JON: It's from our book, it's one of the craziest images. It's a beautiful image that our dear friend Sonia Rentsch, who's a brilliant set designer, put together with our buddy Axel Peemoeller from New Studio. Our buddy Nayquan Shuler took the photo when we were getting in the groove. We shot everything in a week – so many recipes, so many pictures – but we got this one and I was like, 'Alright we onto something, we know the direction.' So this honours that vibe. I feel like as members of a collective, we're different, we approach things differently, so how does that come across in the visuals of the food, because food is not an easy thing to shoot. How do we capture the feeling of Ghetto Gastro?

NELL: Okay, then we have a glass with a cucumber.
JON: That's green juice – just celebrating, honouring the juice bars in our neighbourhood. Green for the money, gold for the honey…eat your greens, drink your greens.
NELL: Are there lots of juice bars in the area?
JON: Yeah, there's a bunch of juice bars in the neighbourhood. These are our health food stores – get your supplements, get your vitamins, get your tonics, juices, smoothies. It's how we stay well.

Photograph by Nayquan Shuler for *Ghetto Gastro Presents Black Power Kitchen* by Jon Gray, Pierre Serrao, Lester Walker with Osayi Endolyn. Artisan Books © 2022

NELL: Then we have a hand with some green leaves…whose hand?
JON: That's Lester holding the collard greens. Collard greens represent abundance. We have collard greens and black eye peas for the new year to represent abundance and good will.
NELL: That's a message that I feel all of you bring across. As you said, there is so much more to Black food than what people think of. Ghetto Gastro always promotes fresh products. It's crazy because you walk around the Lower East Side and people do their weekly shopping in a Wholefoods and spend eighteen dollars on a smoothie to walk home. Obviously pricing like this will exclude people when everyone should have access to fresh and nutritious products.
JON: They're not thinking about us, it's not for us…and I can't blame anybody because it's like, Who's gonna talk to us better than us? That's why we take on that responsibility.

Photograph by Nayquan Shuler for *Ghetto Gastro Presents Black Power Kitchen* by Jon Gray, Pierre Serrao, Lester Walker with Osayi Endolyn. Artisan Books © 2022

NELL: And then we have a scoop of ice cream with fruits and the outline of a body…
JON: Yeah, this is American apple pie, but American with three Ks, because it's representing the destruction and violence towards Black bodies from systems that are supposed to protect us. As American as apple pie, but the funny thing is that apple pie isn't actually an American invention, it's from the French tart. We first crafted this dish when we were working on a project with Hank Willis Thomas for For Freedoms in 2014 or 2015. It was about looking at that FDR speech and thinking about the freedoms and we just wanted to interpret it our way. This is how we flipped it – like you say, we tend to subversive. This is not very subversive, but we tend to make sure things have layers.
NELL: I think that's actually what I was going to say before when I was talking about the group, it's like there's always layers to what you guys do. At the end of the day, you want to eat good food and you want to enjoy it, but there's also layers with you guys. I think that's what drew me to you in the beginning.

Photograph by Nayquan Shuler for *Ghetto Gastro Presents Black Power Kitchen* by Jon Gray, Pierre Serrao, Lester Walker with Osayi Endolyn. Artisan Books © 2022

OPPOSITE AND ABOVE: Gastro x sacai worn by Makki Kowamakkiteia. Photograph by Joshua Woods and styling by Banna Nega

NELL: Now we have Ghetto Gastro x sacai …that's something recent isn't it?
JON: You're getting the first look, this ain't even dropped yet. The pop-up was recent, but the apron is part of the collab that we're doing with sacai – it's coming out May 4th.
NELL: Wait, so you actually have an apron? Or there's a clothing collab?
JON: We got the apron, we got a shirt and the pants, but we didn't have those samples made when we were in Japan doing the pop-ups.
NELL: So how did that collaboration come about?
JON: Organically, you know. Me and my buddy Rocky Xu were in Tokyo in August and we started talking about this space we have with our partners in Tokyo called Burnside and they were like, 'Yeah, we really want to do something at Burnside, but we don't want to do it without Ghetto Gastro'. So we figured it out and in December we took over the streets with sacai Gastro, which we did as a pop-up for the week – waffle variations. Nike partnered with us, and it was lit, so that was the first chapter of the sacai Gastro. Chapter two, Dover Street Market, coming up in May…
NELL: Wait, this is in Dover Street Market, New York or London?
JON: New York.
NELL: Cool, and I guess the other image is around that same time – the blurry face, I think it must be the streets of Tokyo?
JON: Yeah, that's an outtake from that shoot. I just thought it was dope…this brother, he's Sudanese and Japanese. We met on the streets of Tokyo that August – he stopped me and was like, 'Yo, I love what you do'.
NELL: You didn't know each other, and he just stopped you on the street?
JON: Yeah, and then I reached back out when we came out in December. I was like, 'Yeah, we going to work on something, we going to do something,' because I thought he had a great look. We're Black collaborating with the Japanese and he was a representation in human form of what we were doing, the Afro-Asiatic conversation.
NELL: Which brings us back to one of the other pictures that you were talking about before. I wasn't aware of the early trading lines between Africa and Asia.
JON: Yeah, we got to tell those stories.
NELL: And then we have the apron.
JON: Which looks like a durag, so I liked it for that. I thought it was just a dope shot, you know what I'm saying?
NELL: Yeah, definitely. I can't wait to see these; I might start cooking for this apron.
JON: You're going to have to.

Gastro x sacai. Photograph by Joshua Woods and styling by Banna Nega

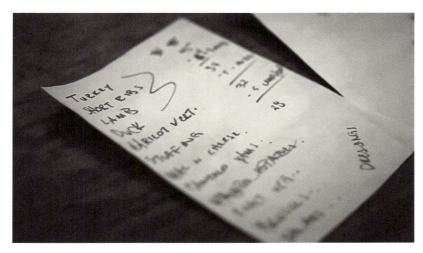

Photograph by Joshua Woods

NELL: Okay, then we have a receipt?
JON: Nah, this is a shopping list that we made when we did the dinner at Rick and Michèle's house [Rick Owens and Michèle Lamy], which was our first project in Paris and opened up the flood gates for us in the fashion game.
NELL: How did that connection come about?
JON: The connection came through this project – our friends Samira Cadesse and Etienne Biloa were working with Rick and Michèle and Samira had known about us, we had met the year before when we went to Paris. When we were on our way to Barbados for a food and rum festival – Samira face-timed me and was with Michèle. This is right after the Bataclan attacks and Michèle was like, 'Hey guys, love what you do, we really want to do something to bring people together, a peaceful, joyous occasion.' Typically they don't celebrate thanksgiving in France but she was like, 'We'll do a thanksgiving for peace,' and that was the project. They had an industrial-style kitchen at their house in France and it just got bust and it turned into a party. It was supposed to be sixty, seventy people but it ended up being like two hundred people. I'm making playlists on the joint with speakers…and that was the beginning of our story.
NELL: So Rick and Michèle were the first ones in the fashion context?
JON: Yeah, Michèle had the vision.
NELL: She's amazing like that, she sees things in people.

Serpentine Pavilion 2018, London, designed by Frida Escobedo
© Frida Escobedo, Taller de Arquitectura. Photograph by Rafael Gamo

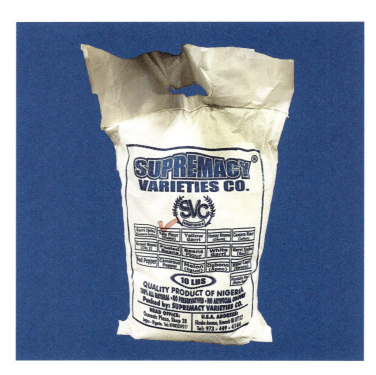

NELL: The next one is Supremacy Varieties Co.
JON: It's basically mashed yam. We did a project at the Serpentine Gallery with Frida Escobedo. It was all about who defines the centre of the world and time, and we were like, Alright the movement of people, colonialism, movement of ingredients. And we looked at the yam as a linchpin that represents some of those things, because the name 'yam' is from Africa, but it's also used in America, but what we call yams in America aren't actually yams, they're sweet potatoes.
NELL: Oh, I did not know that.

TOP: Jennifer Packer, *Blessed Are Those Who Mourn (Breonna! Breonna!)*, 2020, oil on canvas, 299.7 x 438.2 cm
© Jennifer Packer, courtesy of Sikkema Jenkins & Co., New York; Corvi-Mora, London
BOTTOM: Firelei Báez, *Untitled (Carte de l'Isle de Saint Domingue)*, 2022, oil and acrylic on archival printed canvas,
172.7 x 218.4 cm. Image courtesy of the artist and James Cohan, New York
Photograph by Jackie Furtado

Sign for the Black Panther Party's Free Breakfast Program

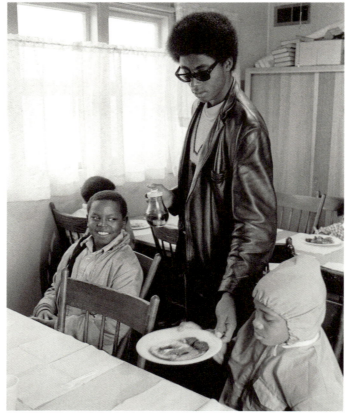

The Black Panther Party's Free Breakfast for
Children Program at St. Augustine's Church, Oakland, 1969.
Photograph by Stephen Shames/Polaris

NELL: You've also supplied us with a list and some images of things that inspire you.
JON: Yeah, there's an image from the Black Panther Breakfast Program – that really inspires the work that we do. Aja Monet's a brilliant poet – Dream Hampton's a great friend. The visual approach in *Belly* by Hype Williams really, really inspired. For me, that was the early work of art where I'm like, Oh I feel like I'm represented in a way that's fresh and fly – it just felt right. You know that scene where they're walking in the strip club and it's like they're glowing? I really like Torkwase Dyson – she's just released a sculpture in the desert in the Coachella Valley, the Desert X, and Toyin Ojih Odutola and Cheyenne Julien.
NELL: And *The Taste of Country Cooking*?
JON: Edna Lewis, she's just one of the OG's that does food.

Simone Leigh, *Cupboard*, 2022, bronze and gold, 225 × 216 × 114.3 cm
Courtesy of the artist and Matthew Marks Gallery
Installation view, the Institute of Contemporary Art/Boston, 2023. Photograph by Timothy Schenck

Lynette Yiadom-Boakye, *The Merry Aces*, 2022, oil on linen, 130 x 200 x 3.7 cm
Courtesy of the Artist, Corvi-Mora, London and Jack Shainman Gallery, New York

Wangechi Mutu, *In Two Canoe*, 2022. Installation view,
Storm King Art Center, New York. Courtesy of the artist and
Gladstone Gallery. Photograph by David Regen

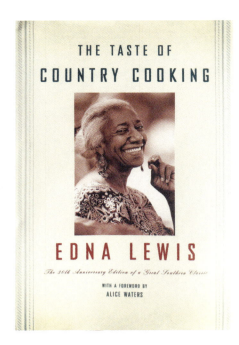

The Taste of Country Cooking
by Edna Lewis

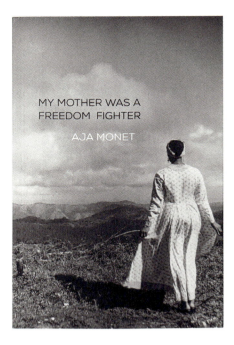

My Mother Was a Freedom Fighter
by Aja Monet

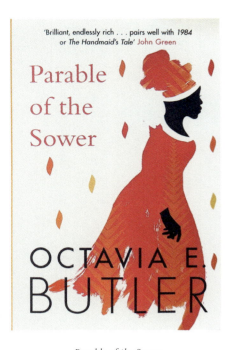

Parable of the Sower
by Octavia E. Butler

Cheyenne Julien, *It Happens Around This Time*, 2022, oil on canvas, 152.4 x 121.9 cm
Courtesy of the artist and Chapter NY, New York. Photograph by Charles Benton

Film stills from *Belly*, 1998, by Hype Williams

CLASSICS

PZtoday, *A Spoon Chair*, 2023
Photograph by Haotian Wang

ULYSSES 100

Paintings and a Poem by

ART HUGHES

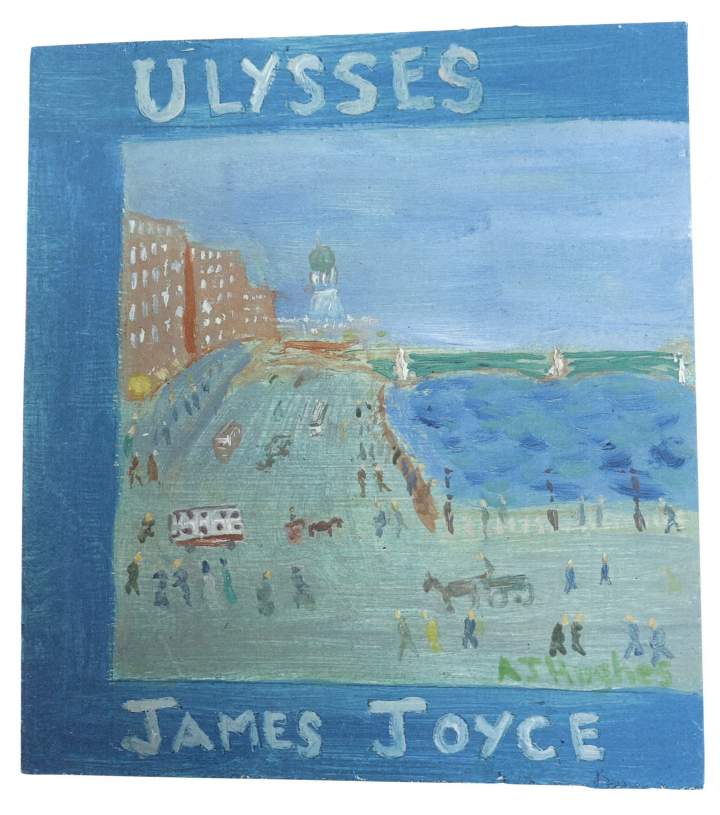

Art Hughes, *Ulysses*, 2022, oil on board, 20.5 x 18 cm

Based at Ulster University, Dr Art Hughes is a Gaelic scholar, broadcaster, writer and artist. In this edition of Luncheon he presents a metrical synopsis of James Joyce's Ulysses, *translated from his original Gaelic poem of the same title. He also includes two oils he has designed for Joyce's* Ulysses *and* A Portrait of the Artist as a Young Man.

I
Golden novel, soul twin,
Joyce's old world, Dublin;
day trip, cut meat, prime,
music, upbeat, sweet-chime.

II
Dubliner, not Gael or Pale,
no son of Rome, no church-tale;
Nation, flung now bother wars,
mother sow young devours.

III
One day's sojourn, bulging seam,
beaming day, June sixteen;
sunny walk, room in tram,
Dedalus, Bloom – stock of Jew-man.

IV
Harbour side, Dublin south,
watchtower grey, stone-mouth;
singing, shaving hair of beard,
Mulligan, raving, stair appeared.

V
Steven, History class, the school,
Deasy's lecture, pay-tool;
Sandymount, sought a while,
lonely thought in stockpile.

VI
Blustery Bloom, jumps to feet,
busty Molly, drowse-sleep;
each their pain, each their post,
Bloom's vain speech uppermost.

VII
Bloom scans lover texts;
Dignam then and last respects;
bitter rue, aghast, sad wail,
Jew, outcast, Gentile-Pale.

VIII
Major moment, man to man,
Stephen, Bloom in *Freeman*;
business, cater, bills to pay,
spills out later speech-play.

IX
Byrne's, lunch, quiet drink,
afternoon for free-think.
Conjure bright doll, if you will,
Moll' on height by Howth-hill.

X
Shakespeare, wealth and seed,
National Library, group-read;
spouses' rights, bard Will's wile,
spills out hard in free-style.

XI
Good king Hamlet set in frame,
drama, tension, end-game;
talk of beds, chattels, stock,
Mulligan rattles, poppycock.

XII
Ormond, drinks, talk, pep,
Boylan's slinking sidestep.
Molly's room, sure of bed:
poor Bloom's very homestead.

XIII
Dedalus with Dollard pure
Love's Sweet Song, Bloom allure;
from life's sling, Heaven's sake,
wife's fling a heartbreak.

XVIII

Bloom, boom, maternity cot,
raucous youth and claptrap;
life's joyish, bitter reel,
boyish skitter, lust-spiel.

XIX

Burke's pub, Buck and Bloom,
hammer, tongs in backroom.
Smother night not on list
"You might another, I insist!"

XIV

Martha, letter – evening mail;
Kernan's pub beyond curtail:
Citizen's bawling broad,
brawling for the downtrod!

XV

Little mutt comes to heel
fluent Gaelic, dog-spiel.
Hey presto, boyhood hurl
manifesto, joy-food unfurl.

XVI

Bloom pits force and might,
defending ancient Israelite;
nation holy, brave and bold,
crave for lowly Leopold!

XVII

Cunningham's carriage, beach,
Gerty MacDowell, crave-peach;
Bloom must, glee in bower,
lust of bee for white-flower.

XX

Whorehouse, visit, strident con,
yearn for flesh and turn-on,
seated smarter, weak at knees
garter, peak and lace-tease.

XXI

Stephen's mother – spectre, grave,
haunting vision, night-rave;
female Hamlet, partake woe,
heartache, candid outflow.

XXII

Higgins, Cohen, also Kitty,
piano, Bloom, sheet, pert-titty.
Army, goading – cutting rough,
butting, boding, fisticuff.

XIII

Bloom to rescue, beady eye
bonding, bun, drivers' layby;
wounds licked, pardoned fault,
wit of hardened Sea-salt.

XXIV

Bloom's house, short the walk,
secrets shared and soul-talk;
Stephen weak, soon to leave,
Bloom in sneak to silk-sleeve.

XXV

Morning fire, passion's blaze,
Molly swoons in lust-haze,
lippy smile, flushed of face,
hippy, guile-rushed yearn-race.

XXVI

Soliloquy, open, naked bare,
sexual, strident, fun-of-fare;
brave, embolden, free from grovel,
Ulysses golden, wonder-novel!

/ Golden novel

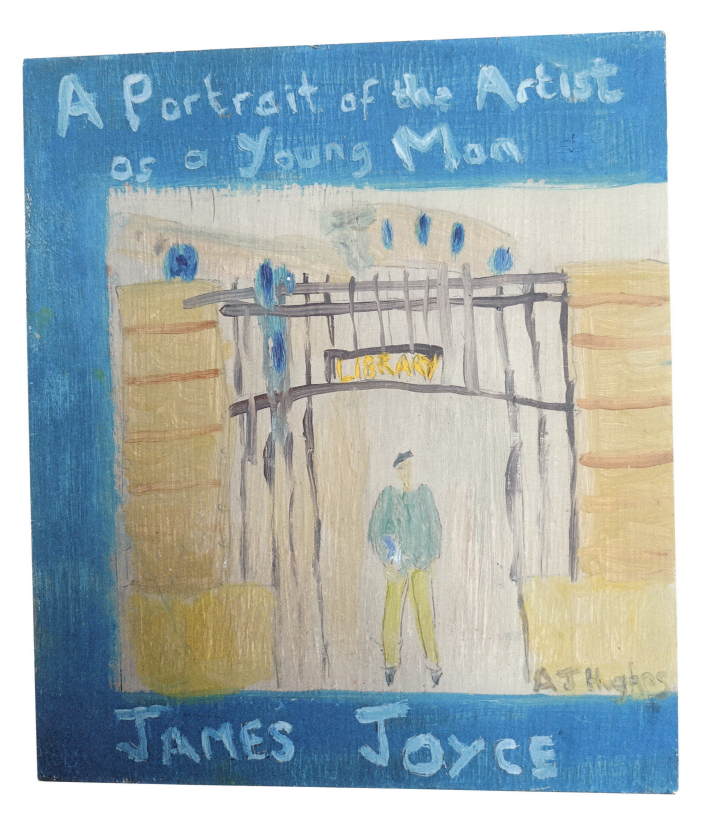

Art Hughes, *A Portrait of the Artist as a Young Man,* 2022, oil on board, 19.5 x 16.5 cm

PZtoday, *Paris is Burning*, 2023

DESSERTS

PZtoday, *Paris is Burning*, 2023
Photograph by Erick Faulkner, Le Dauphin restaurant, Paris

LIGHTS AROUND

All clothes throughout by COMME DES GARÇONS, AW23

PHOTOGRAPHS BY PAOLO ROVERSI
STYLING BY ROBBIE SPENCER

Model SIHANA SHALAJ at IMG

Hair Stylist TOMOHIRO OHASHI at MA GROUP • *Make-Up Artist* MARIE DUHART at BRYANT ARTIST
Manicurist TYPHAINE KERSUAL at ARTISTS UNIT • *Set Designer* JEAN HUGUES DE CHATILLON
Casting Director PIERGIORGIO DEL MORO of DMCASTING and HELENA BALLADINO for DMCASTING

Photography Assistant CLARA BELLEVILLE and CHIARA VITTORINI
Styling Assistant JOSEPH ECORCHARD • *Hair Stylist Assistant* XIAOYUAN YANG • *Make-Up Assistant* LOU BOIDEN
Digital Operator MARIE AMELIE MARTIN • *Production* STUDIO DEMI

With very special thanks to REI KAWAKUBO and ADRIAN JOFFE.
And to Marilyn Porlan, Anna Hägglund, Silvia Sini and Jeanne Schmitt

Shaped polyester dress with flowered knots and synthetic slip-on platform sneakers by COMME DES GARÇONS × SALOMON
Opposite: Shaped dress with flowered knots in polyester and synthetic slip-on platform sneakers by COMME DES GARÇONS × SALOMON
Headpiece by VALERIANE VENANCE FOR COMME DES GARÇONS

'WHATEVER THE SITUATION, EVEN WITH NO MATERIALS NOR SPACE, I CAN MAKE SOMETHING JUST WITH WHAT IS AROUND ME, IF I WANT TO MAKE IT FROM MY HEART.

SO IF I THINK ABOUT MAKING CLOTHES THAT NOBODY ELSE HAS MADE, I CAN DO IT. I CAN FIND THE WAY.'

— REI KAWAKUBO
APRIL 2023

Opposite: Wool jacket, and dress with spiral forms and cotton shoes. Wig by TAKEO ARAI FOR COMME DES GARÇONS

Nylon dress and synthetic slip-on platform sneakers by COMME DES GARÇONS × SALOMON
Opposite: Shaped polyester dress with flowered knots and synthetic slip-on platform sneakers by COMME DES GARÇONS × SALOMON

Acrylic fur coat
Opposite: Acrylic fur coat, dress and cotton shoes

Polyester dress
Opposite: Flat dress in wool
Previous Spread: Headpiece by VALERIANE VENANCE FOR COMME DES GARÇONS

COUTURE

PHOTOGRAPHS BY **NADINE IJEWERE**
STYLING BY **NELL KALONJI**

Model **DIVINE MUGISHA** at STORM

Hair Stylist **AKEMI KISHIDA** at MA GROUP • Make-Up Artist **AURORE GIBRIEN** at BRYANT ARTISTS • Nail Artist **CAM TRAN** at ARTLIST
Set Designer **MANON EVERHARD** at STREETERS • Casting Director **ANITA BITTON** at ESTABLISHMENT
Movement Director **BENJAMIN JONSSON** at BOX ARTIST MANAGEMENT • Post-production **BEN PICKETT** at TOUCH

Photography Assistants **JORDAN LEE** and **KOBY BOAFO** • Styling Assistant **HONOR DANGERFIELD** and **WINNIE REILLY**
Hair Stylist Assistant **TSUYOSHI TAMAI** • Make-Up Assistant **LOU BOIDON** • Set Design Assistants **LEO PENVEN** and **MARIE GRIHON**
Digital Technician **ZOE SALT** • Production CLM

Opposite: Jersey high-neck bodysuit and couture maxi skirt in crispy lurex taffeta by ALAÏA

Asymmetric black crepe wool dress by JEAN PAUL GAULTIER COUTURE BY HAIDER ACKERMANN
Opposite: Black lace dress embellished with mirror sequins and an embroidered plastron with bird motifs by MONTEX FOR CHANEL and ankle boots in golden leather by MASSARO FOR CHANEL

Shaped tailored wool jacket enhanced with hand-painted irregular tennis ecru stripes, organic cotton shirt, wool tie and pleated trousers and shoes by SCHIAPARELLI HAUTE COUTURE SS23

Gazar bustier dress and skirt with accordion pleats by ARMANI PRIVÉ SS13

Tuxedo coat over burnished radzimir top and skirt by DIOR HAUTE COUTURE
Opposite: Cape brodée robe by CELINE COUTURE BY HEDI SLIMANE

Long dress entirely embroidered with ostrich and coquetips feathers by GIAMBATTISTA VALLI HAUTE COUTURE

Technical cut-out dress by VALENTINO LE CLUB COUTURE
Opposite: Sequin embroidered recycled nylon donut jacket, sequin embroidered stretch denim athena gown, long leather gloves and leather flared platform boots by RICK OWENS

SCARECROWS

The idea was to start the year in a fitting way. This series of photographs by Estelle Hanania, styled by Léopold Duchemin, presents the inaugural project facing the first-year costume design students at the Paul Poiret school in Paris when they were fresh out of high school. The scarecrow, *l'épouvantail* in French, could be the ultimate costume. It's designed to be an instrument of horror (and being asked to work with a straw bale can be quite scary for an eighteen year old). The scarecrow speaks for, and stands by, itself. However, the students left a corridor of empty space in the midst of their chaff effigies to welcome the performer Helena de Laurens, bringing the straw, nets and bundles to life as characters. – Zoé Wirgin

All works by costume design students from the Paul Poiret school in Paris

Costume by LÉONIE RENOUD

PHOTOGRAPHS BY ESTELLE HANANIA
STYLING BY LÉOPOLD DUCHEMIN

PROJECT LED BY ZOÉ WIRGIN
AT LYCÉE PAUL POIRET, STATE SCHOOL FOR FASHION
AND PERFORMING ARTS, PARIS.

Worn by HELENA DE LAURENS

Hair Stylist MICHAEL DELMAS at TOTAL MANAGEMENT • *Make-Up Artist* ANTHONY PREEL at ARTLIST
Styling Assistant ESTHER TALABER

Costume by **FANNY COPÉRÉ**

Costume by MARIE NICOLLE

Costume by KAYNA RIBEYROL

Costume by ANNA L'HOSTIS

Costume by MAX-AENGUS BUREL

Costume by AGNÈS SANDOZ

Costume by ROSE KOWALSKI

Costume by ROSE KOWALSKI

Costume by CAMILLE BONNEAU

Costume by BLANCHE GROSSOCORDONE

Costume by ENORA LAPEYRE

Costume by FANNY COPÉRÉ

Costume by LÉONIE RENOUD

Costume by JULIETTE ROUAS

Costume by ISAURE TRÉTOUT

Costume by CLARA BESNARD

BY THE WATER'S EDGE

PHOTOGRAPHS BY **JEANO EDWARDS**
STYLING BY **HISATO TASAKA**

Models **MAJDA JOHN PETER** at ELITE and **MIMI ANGETH** at THE SQUAD

Hair Stylist **RIMI URA** at CALLISTÉ AGENCY
Casting Director **PEOPLE-FILE** at MINI TITLE • *Production* WEBBER REPRESENTS

Opposite: Mimi wears T-Shirt by **THE ANIMALS OBSERVATORY**, cropped mohair patchwork polo shirt by **MARNI**
and silk scarf as a skirt by **HERMÈS**

Majda wears Java beaded macramé cotton dress by **WALES BONNER** and leather shoes by **JOHN LOBB**
Opposite: Mimi wears knitted cotton vest by **BABAÀ** and Java beaded macramé cotton dress by **WALES BONNER**

Majda wears faux-fur coat by CELINE BY HEDI SLIMANE and model's own jewellery
Opposite: Mimi wears crochet top by DRIES VAN NOTEN

Mimi wears T-shirt by THE ANIMALS OBSERVATORY, cropped mohair patchwork polo shirt by MARNI, silk scarf as a skirt by HERMÈS and sneakers by ADIDAS
Majda wears T-Shirt by MARINE SERRE, silk scarf as a skirt by HERMÈS and sneakers by ADIDAS
Opposite: Mimi wears printed silk dress by PRADA

Mimi wears shirt and dress by LEMAIRE, jeans by BLUEMARBLE
and leather shoes by JOHN LOBB
Opposite: Majda wears maxi-mesh cotton and cashmere turtleneck
jumper by HERMÈS, skirt by MAME KUROGOUCHI
and model's own jewellery

Mimi wears printed silk dress by PRADA
Opposite: Majda wears maxi-mesh cotton and cashmere turtleneck jumper by HERMÈS, skirt by MAME KUROGOUCHI, sneakers by ADIDAS and model's own jewellery

Majda wears cropped mohair patchwork polo shirt by MARNI
Opposite: Majda wears cropped mohair patchwork polo shirt by MARNI and trousers by JUNYA WATANABE MAN

Majda wears knitted dress by ISSEY MIYAKE, top and dress by MAME KUROGOUCHI and leather shoes by JOHN LOBB
Opposite: Mimi wears knitted cotton vest by BABAÀ and Java beaded macramé cotton dress by WALES BONNER

NEW YORK NEW YORK
A BOTTLE AND A CORK

PHOTOGRAPHS BY CRUZ VALDEZ
STYLING BY MARCUS CUFFIE

Models NYA BUOM at STATE MANAGEMENT and MELL at NEXT

Hair Stylist SONNY MOLINA at STREETERS using DAVINES • *Make-Up Artist* JANESSA PARÉ at THE GOOD COMPANY
Casting Director NICO MAO at MIDLAND CASTING

Photography Assistants FERNANDO CEREZO and SEBASTIAN ACERO
Styling Assistant JACOB ACE • *Production* CLM

Mell wears half zipped cotton bomber jacket by WILLY CHAVARRIA, satin split skirt
skirt by VAQUERA, model's own boxers and sunglasses by ILLESTEVA
Opposite: Nya wears caschot cadel coat, leather scarf and gloves by THE ROW and sunglasses by ILLESTEVA
Following Spread: Nya wears polyester scarf by ECKHAUS LATTA, cotton coat by CDLM, sunglasses by ILLESTEVA
Nya wears cotton dress by CDLM, darted wool bodysuit, maxi flare skirt and leather boots by MARC JACOBS

Mell wears cotton jumbo hoodie and wide leg jeans by R13, silk printed dress by SC103
Opposite: Mell wears cotton shirt and hat by R3DELICTE, cotton shirt and tie by A--COMPANY
Following Spread: Nya wears mesh logo bodysuit by AREA, long fringe polyester bra by VAQUERA, wide leg jeans by R13 and shoes by MANOLO BLAHNIK

Mell wears leather pea coat by COACH
Opposite: Nya wears printed silk dress by CHRISTOPHER JOHN ROGERS and leather half gloves by VAQUERA

Mell wears cotton fur lined jacket by MARC JACOBS, mesh titty twister top by VAQUERA, crossover jeans by R13
Opposite: Nya wears cotton angry dog dress by GIOVANNA FLORES, leather half gloves and fringe belt by VAQUERA

Nya wears wool and leather dress by GABRIELA HEARST
Opposite: Nya wears mesh and cotton polo cape by CDLM

THE HOLES IN MY SWEATER

PHOTOGRAPHS BY BHUMIKA SHARMA
STYLING BY MANGLIEN GANGTE

Models JODEE GUITE, JOUKIM KHONGSAI, RAHUL RAI, KHUP HANGSING, C. SAILO and VANEESRI KAUL TYAGI

Opposite: Jodee wears stylist's own shirt and their grandmother's textile as a skirt

CD gifted by Vaneesri's grandfather. Portrait of Rahul's grandfather
Opposite: Joukim wears their own shirt, grandmother's jacket and trousers from BYGONE ECHOES

Premayni, a book by Rahul's grandfather
Opposite: Rahul wears stylist's own trousers

Jodee and Joukim wear their own clothes

Khup wears their own top and scarf knitted by them and their friend

Opposite: C. Sailo wears their own T-Shirt, trousers by **BYGONE ECHOES**, stylist's own scarf and a handwritten playlist from an old lover

A picture of an old toothbrush left by C. Sailo's lover at his place
Opposite: Vaneesri wears their grandfather's old suit

LUNCHEON
MASTHEAD

TOP TABLE
Editor and Publisher Frances Armstrong Jones
Guest Fashion Director Nell Kalonji
Managing Editor Josefine Skomars
Art Directors Giulia Garbin and Mariana Sameiro
Consultant Text Editor/Production Advisor Sophie Kullmann
Contributing Editor Charlie Porter
Contributing Editor Reginald Moore
Associate Publisher Buzio Saraiva assisted by Anne-Christine Caro
Fashion/Editorial Assistant Max Kallio
Accounting Ben Warren

SPECIAL THANKS TO
Joanna Allison, Yo Arakida, Harriet Balfour, Silvia Baltschun, Alexandre Baret, Helen Barr, Max Bellhouse, Piera Berardi, Aldo Bettazzi, Dickon Bowden, Charlie and Kate Boxer, Jackson Boxer, Jessica Burke, Anne-Christine Caro, Gareth Casey, Marie Chaix, Sarah Chatto, Hannah Chinn, Pauline Cochet-Dallet, Honor Dangerfield, Hugh Corcoran, Chloe Ellis, Ginevra Elkann, Alexander Fang, Kerry Francis, Janet Fischgrund, Hannah George, James Gilchrist, Phoebe Greenwood, Stewart Grimshaw, Michael and Lisa Lindsay-Hogg, Fergus and Margot Henderson, Daisy Hoppen, Anna Hägglund, Adrian Joffe, Iva Keselicová, Paolina Leccese, Yilin Ma, Olivia Manousaridou, Amalie Marinas, Myles Mansfield, Maud, Astrid Meek, Lucie and Luke Meier, Boris Meister, Erdem Moralioglu, Freya Morris, Eric Namont, Duro Olowu, Nathalie Ours, Owen Parry, Lola Peploe, Tom Penn, Marilyn Porlan, Richard Porter, Anu Purmonen, Colette Randall, Francois Ravard, Rex, Sally Robotham, Theresa Romualdez, Rose Bakery, Paolo Roversi, Leslie Simitch, Henrik and Tina Skomars, Jamila-Lee Smikle, Lucy Snowdon, Isla Sofia and Patrick Stevenson-Keating, Sybil, Melissa Thompson, Monica Truong, Marco Velardi, Grace Wales Bonner, Naoki Watanabe, Yasuhiro Watanabe, Richard Windsor, Zach Wolff, Angharad Wood

Thank you sincerely to everyone who has contributed in large or small ways to this issue. These pages are yours. I would like to dedicate this issue to Charlie Porter with much love. And to the memory of Maureen Doherty with infinite gratitude. Xx Frances

PRINTING AND PREPRESS
Luncheon Magazine is printed at Graphius, Ghent, Belgium. With the much appreciated support of Kevin Ward. Prepress by Dexter Premedia with the much appreciated support of Richard Deal and Dan Kosta. *Luncheon* is typeset using Bembo, Perpetua, Sackers Gothic Std by Monotype and English Egyptian by Abyme.

COPYRIGHT
Published twice a year by Luncheon Magazine Ltd. Copyright Luncheon Magazine Ltd. All rights reserved. No part of this publication may be reproduced in whole or part without written permission from the publisher. Every reasonable effort has been made to trace copyright holders, but if any have been inadvertently overlooked, the necessary arrangements will be made at the first opportunity. The views expressed in *Luncheon* are those of the respective contributors and are not necessarily shared by *Luncheon* and its staff. The magazine welcomes new contributions but can assume no responsibility for unsolicited manuscripts, photographs, illustrations or art work.

FOUNDERS
Frances Armstrong Jones and Thomas Persson

CONTACT
contact@luncheonmagazine.com
www.luncheonmagazine.com

DISTRIBUTION
Worldwide Distribution
KD PRESSE – Alexandre Baret
alexandre@kdpresse.com
+33 142 46 02 20

Luncheon is printed on Munken Polar (by Arctic paper) which is FSC and EU Ecolabel certified. Munken is an environmentally friendly and ecologically sound paper produced at Munkedals in Sweden, which is one of the world's cleanest fine paper mills.
Graphius uses vegetable inks for the printing of *Luncheon*, partly powered by solar panels.

Looks good - feels great - doesn't kill you - choose MARFA - out now
Photograph by Theo Sion, London 2022

LUNCHEON
MAGAZINE ARCHIVE

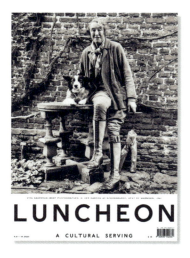

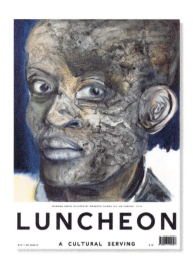

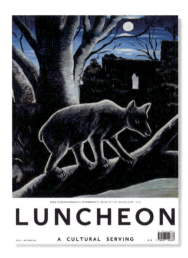

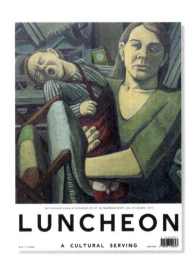

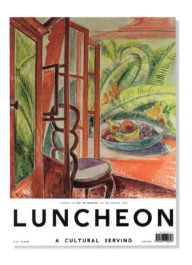
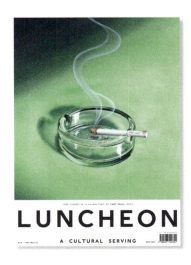

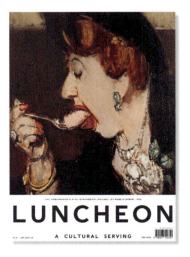

LUNCHEON
EDITIONS

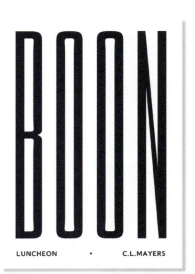

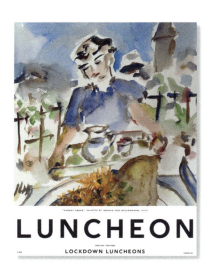

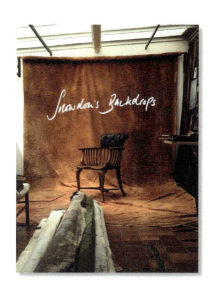

JORDAN HEMINGWAY

DEATH OF A MOUNTAIN

PUBLISHED BY
LUNCHEON EDITIONS
AVAILABLE AT THE LUNCHEON KIOSK
AT DOVER STREET MARKET
MAY 2O23

LUNCHEON
THINGS

**LUNCHEON T-SHIRT
WITH CIGARETTE DRAWING
BY ROBERT WYATT**

Installation at Dover Street Market, December 2022

PZtoday, *Coffee Necklaces*, 2023

DIGESTIFS

PZtoday, *Coffee Necklaces*, 2023
Antony Tsykin photographed by Erick Faulkner at Le Dauphin

A SHORT NO STORY

BY
HUGH CORCORAN
PAINTING BY
PETER DOYLE

Peter Doyle, *A Short No Story*, 2023, acrylic on canvas
Photograph by Alex Tracey

It was the evening of a Saturday. The rain continued to pour down outside on the cold Parisian streets as I watched from the warm interior of the bar counter whilst freeing myself of a heavy coat and scarf. I hung the articles on a coat hanger by the door and returned to my high stool to say hello. A glass of sparkling wine was set on the counter and then pushed in my direction with no indication of the fact that it was for me, other than that discreet motion. I took it gladly and thanked the man who offered it to me. His name was Phillipe, but he was more commonly known as Pinouche, for reasons I never asked about. His demeanour was controlled, each movement was considered and completed in its own good time. A cork was pulled gently from its bottle neck, barely making a sound. The cork is raised slowly to the nose and sniffed at. All is well. A little wine is poured out into a glass and tasted, Pinouche looks into himself, pauses and thinks. It seems good, he lifts a round carafe and pours the cloudy, reddish liquid with a slight purple hue violently into the empty vessel. It is swirled around and shook up before leaving for its table.

The evening light has now faded and the darkness outside and teeming rain accentuate the protection of the clean, well-lit room. The telephone rings and Pinouche exhales a sigh of frustration, rolling his eyes, and answers 'Oui?'

He waits for a response.

'No, I'm sorry, if you want a table for the 14th of April, you must call me on the 10th of April. I cannot take this booking now.'

Another moment passes.

'Why?!' he asks the voice behind the telephone. 'Because I am not sure whether or not I will be dead by then. Voilà, merci, adieu.' He replaces the telephone onto its receiver and looks as if to remember what he had been doing.

Charles, his waiter, standing in the background polishing glasses, laughs to himself. A dry smile can be seen on Pinouche's face as he returns to the book of poems he was reading and sips his glass of wine.

In the back of the room lies a kitchen in which three people work with concentration and rigour. A small, spectacled older lady with cropped, greying hair who is impressive and beautiful; a taller, larger man with a bald head and the look of a bricklayer; and a slight, thin, dark-skinned man who is unassuming and quietly skimming stock. None of them are young.

The woman's name is Raquel, she is the owner and matriarch of the little bistro in which I am sitting. She came here from Argentina, via Mexico and Italy, while escaping the fascist dictatorship to which she was actively opposed and opened the modest restaurant over three decades ago.

The larger of the two men is Jerôme, a Frenchman, he has worked here for over twenty years and he is a loyal man who has never let them down in all that time. And the third is Lalith, from Sri Lanka, who has been here for a decade or more and who first came to this city alone, hoping to one day be joined by his wife and daughter.

I sip my glass and watch the handwritten blackboard with its chalk-etched calligraphy, each word carefully drawn out in beautiful old French lettering. Veal brains, chitterlings, fish broth, barbajuans, crêpes with tomato sauce, mackerel tartare, oysters, pork terrine, roast chicken, poached beef cheeks, sweetbreads in lemon butter, pigeon cooked two ways, monkfish and olives.

Pinouche asks if I am ready to order. I ask for the brains and the monkfish. As I speak, the beautiful calligraphy of the blackboard is recreated on the docket in ink. Charles, who acts like a photographer's assistant, takes the docket and brings it to the kitchen. I hear my name being mentioned as the paper is handed in, table numbers being replaced by names of regular customers here.

I ask if I could order some wine.

'Would you like a bottle or a glass?' is the response.

Always a bottle of course, unless I'm ill perhaps, but it is appropriate to ask the question at least.

'Red, or white?'

'I'm not sure, something good.' A sigh of frustration again.

'Well I can't read your mind, what do you want, red or white?' He's not in the mood to guess.

'Okay white.'

'D'accord.' Pinouche turns his back and rummages around in the fridge, ponders, goes downstairs, comes back. Has a think, then says, 'I have a little Chenin Blanc if you wish.'

'Of course, that would be lovely. Thank you.'

The wine is discreetly uncorked, tasted, carafed and put in front of me to taste.

'Does that please you?'

'It is excellent. What is it?' I ask.

The bottle is set in front of me to examine. A simple label with not much information. The bottle is, unbeknown to me, quite rare. I have never been introduced to it or seen it. I will later learn of its rarity. For now, I will quietly drink, take pleasure and no one will comment on how rare it is to be served this bottle. It is treated as if I had been served a bottle of house white. 'If you don't ask, you don't get' isn't an idiom which has any use or sense in this establishment.

The food arrives, slightly under-seasoned in what I believe to be a considerate gesture to the diner to add a little salt at the end if they so wish, but avoiding the disappointing event of an over-seasoned plate which leaves them dehydrated and saturated. I add a little *fleur de sel* and drink the deeply mineral, rich white wine to quench my thirst.

I pass comment to Pinouche who has no interest in small talk. Only when I approach the subject of poetry or literature is he willing to engage seriously in conversation. Dry wit and humour dapple his dure demeanour. A portrait of Beckett hangs on the wall to the right of the bar. It is a rare photograph of Beckett laughing. Those who do not understand Beckett usually have not understood his humour, the same can be said for Pinouche.

Charles, the photographer's assistant, helps to lighten the mood and reassure me that I am more than welcome here, smiling, asking me if I need anything, passing me a glass to try and ruffling my hair as he passes through the small dining room.

I sit quietly eating my meal, chatting from time to time, a book folded in one hand. The absence of piped music, that thing that fills all our public and private spaces now, allows me to concentrate on my book or on the din and hum of diners conversing, lifting glasses and replacing them, knives and forks clinking on plates, chairs being pulled in and out across the tiled floor, bottles being opened, and pots and pans being moved around.

The wine dims my senses and I can no longer concentrate on my book, so I fold over the corner and place it into my jacket pocket. I am tired after dinner and the wine has made me jolly. I politely chat to a customer I know at the bar; the conversation is shared, the staff participate. I pour the man a glass from my bottle, he thanks me and holds up his hand to tell me not to give him too much. A man laughs a little loudly and I watch as he is glared at from behind the counter. A couple ask for coffees and the bill, they catch each other's glance then and kiss. Another couple arrive to ask if there might be a table available. 'Sorry, not tonight.'

Charles, having danced around the house all night, steps outside for a cigarette. All the main courses have been served. He is tall and handsome and has wild, thick and unkempt hair which at times stands up on his head. He is good at his job, and although he is aware of this he sometimes wonders if others are too. He remembers every wine each customer has drank, and those who come back in two months only need to ask to be reminded. His politeness and boyish charm open doors for him and set the room at ease. But he is restless and sometimes, after a long week, will disappear into the night for a day or two to forget about it all. At 29 years old he laments the loss of a world he's never lived in and stays true to the ideals of another generation who 'demanded no water for the table but rather ordered a bottle of *grand cru* for their meal and a Beaujolais Village to quench their thirst'.

Now the room is audibly calmer. The nervous chatter of hungry people has been replaced by the slow and tired conversation of the well-fed and tipsy. Small talk has been replaced by storytelling, jokes and long-winded proposals and debates. Those within the kitchen are slowly cleaning, but the sound and smell of cleaning is overshadowed by the talkative diners, each private conversation too being masked and protected by the general clatter.

Raquel emerges from her workshop sporting a silk neckerchief and apron. She does not ask anyone did they enjoy their meals or search for compliments, but quietly collects plates and polite diners thank her for the meal. She smiles humbly and thanks them. At her age most people in France have retired, yet she continues to work each day in an act of Titan sacrifice for her customers. Even now she still experiments and attempts to invent new desserts or try new recipes, unrelenting to the onward march of time. But on her days off she grows roses in her garden, and she has told me, on an evening such as this one, that had she been anything else but a cook she would have liked to be a gardener.

When cheese has been sliced off the wheel, which lies upon a wooden table near the kitchen, and chocolate fondants, crème brulées, ice creams and shortbreads have been served, she comes to the bar to join her partner Pinouche. She pours a glass of red wine and takes a drink and chats to him about the night. He looks back at her with none of the severity he saves for others, his stance and stare now gentle and kind.

Almost a quarter of a century ago, they met in a bar not unlike this one. He had tried to buy her a drink but she refused, buying him one instead. He turned to the barman, after the mysterious and beautiful woman had left him, and asked who she was.

'Oh, you don't know Raquel?' he answered. 'Well, she runs a little bistro like this one, except the food is much better.' He decided to go and see her in her little bistro. And now here he stands beside her, watching her with all the awe and affection he did on that first night.

Finally, the diners filter out into the dark of the night, coats are put on, collars turned up, scarves wrapped around shoulders, goodbyes said, and bills paid.

The room is now much quieter than before, save the odd sound of a pot being arranged somewhere in the kitchen. Cigarettes are lit at the bar and ashtrays provided. There is a light sound of conversation as the workers and some regulars finish off saying what must be said. I ask what Le Baratin means anyway. There is a pause while they think. An example, you can hear baratin at the bar, or at the market, simple chit-chat among friends. Here we talk, we eat, we drink, we meet. What happens? Nothing happens. 'A short story about nothing. No, no, that's not right,' Pinouche wonders. 'A short no-story,' he decides.